# Leader Reader One

## Authentic Lessons in Leadership

### Lt. Col (Ret) Tom Davis, CRNA

### ProSynEx.com

Copyright 2017 by Thomas Davis
All rights reserved

# Table of Contents

About the Author

Introduction

Getting Started

Foundation of Trust

The Path to Leadership

Leadership Skills

Developing the Mission

Recapping Leadership

References

# ABOUT THE AUTHOR

Lt. Col (Ret.) Tom S. Davis is a respected speaker and healthcare leader, author, AANA Newsbulletin contributor and anesthesia provider. He is the former Chief of the Division of Nurse Anesthesia at The Johns Hopkins Hospital in Baltimore and Chief Nurse Anesthetist at (Baylor) Scott and White Hospital, Main OR in Temple, TX.

Tom developed the first national distance anesthesia education program for CRNA's while a member of the graduate faculty at the University of Kansas Medical Center. At The Johns Hopkins Tom developed the leadership team for the supervision of over 100 CRNAs. Tom's method for value-based hiring was adopted and implemented and he developed and updated the orientation manual to a digital format. Under Tom's leadership the merit-based bonus system was put into place and the annual performance review process was revised. He was on the 2015 faculty for the AANA Fall Leadership Academy, and is a member of the AANA Professional Practice Division Advisory Board and the AANA Foundation Rise Above Committee. He is a Serving Leader trainer with Third River Partners.

As well as speaking regularly for healthcare organizations nationwide, Tom specializes in developing "leadership with civility," team building and workflow, patient-centered safety and value based recruitment and retention. He maintains an active web presence at www.prosynex.com and www.procrna.com.

An avid health and fitness advocate, Tom is a former tri-athlete who has run The Boston Marathon, The Honolulu Marathon, The Bloomsday in Spokane, and routinely cycles the MS 150. Tom and his wife, Liz, have cycled large portions of a dozen Bikeline river "routes" in Germany and Austria, their favorite being the loop-d-loop wine region of the Mosel. They divide their time living in Ellicott City, MD and Temple, TX while dreaming about owning a dog and "living Aloha" in Hawaii.

# Introduction

*"You have to be very careful if you don't know where you are going, because you might not get there." – Yogi Berra*

Some journeys are short and well defined going from point A to B quickly, efficiently and reliably.  My journey through healthcare leadership extends over decades to a destination that did not exist when the trip started.   I didn't hop on a plane in New York on Monday and arrive in LA 5 hours and 52 minutes later the same day.  My flight has lasted over 40 years connecting in Tucson, Tokyo, San Antonio, Baltimore, Spokane and Kansas City.  But the plane never has landed in LA.

As a middle school student I was attracted to the sciences and in high school I felt a draw to healthcare and to the military.  Over the next few years I satisfied two dreams by becoming a Nurse Anesthetist and serving 21 years in the US Air Force.  During my initial training both in anesthesia and as a military officer, I was mentored by people dedicated to empowering others by sharing their knowledge and experience.  Over the length of my ongoing career the latest and greatest way to accomplish a task continued to evolve, but the concepts of teamwork and personal mentoring remained constant.

While being promoted through the military ranks and later into proprietary civilian positions, I remained an avid student of leadership with a deep seated curiosity about why some leaders were more effective than others. Though I have been fortunate to work with many outstanding leaders along the way, I have also worked with leaders driven more by the quest for power than the empowerment of others. As an eternal optimist, I learned valuable lessons from both. I observed that poor leaders were frequently highly competent people who simply lacked training in leadership. And I also learned that things that used to challenge me as a new leader became routine and easily managed if I used the right tools with my integrity intact. As my leadership skills developed, I pledged to mentor those around me so that competent emerging leaders could flourish rather than falter.

*Leader Reader 1, Authentic Lessons in Leadership* is my mentoring gift to the future leaders of the healthcare industry. Healthcare has moved from paper to digital and from X-ray to sophisticated scanners. Communication has moved from memos to digital message boards and personal texting. In the middle of this speed-of-light evolution, effective leadership that connects with team members through personal interaction remains just as important as it did four decades ago, and it will continue to be important decades into the future.

Inside these pages you will find a mentor for your leadership development. Perhaps you will learn why you wanted to be on the leadership pathway, or if you want to be a leader at all. You will begin by reflecting on your own integrity, your vision, your set of values and the ways in which those natural characteristics can or should be changed in order to lead successfully. Through the stories of other healthcare leaders and historic figures, and a few sports legends we all know well, you will witness success and failure, promotion and replacement, leadership behaviors that work and those that don't. You will be introduced to honest, transparent folks and opaque power-seekers. And by the end of the book you will reflect on ethical character and the role of personality and communication skills. You will respect the importance of being organized, of building trust, of having a productive meeting, of the critical need to continue to learn and the fairness of mentoring others. You'll reflect often and remember a lot.

When I started this trip to leadership, I was headed in a general direction without a charted course. By now I am a seasoned traveler and a frequent flyer on a journey that is still young. *Leader Reader 1* is the guide that would have made my journey so much easier. I invite you join me on this continuing adventure. There's an empty seat by the window.

*"Success is never final and failure never fatal. It's courage that counts."*

**Mike Ditka, NFL coach**

# Chapter 1

# Getting Started

*"Successful leaders turn dreams and plans into action and reality."*

Every autumn Universities across the nation start a new cohort of students on the pathway to licensing and certification in a variety of healthcare professions. Selection committees are confident that they have chosen the elite among the applicants. But with the start of the semester, the thrill of having been selected is replaced with uncertainty and at some point almost every student will ask, "Can I do it?" An empathetic faculty will reassure students that they have been thoughtfully selected not because of what they know, but because of their ability to learn, and that they will be challenged to use that ability to learn something new every day. Students are urged to trust that by the end of training in their selected fields of study, they will be ready to work independently.

A new leader in healthcare isn't much different than a new university student. You, too, may have a combination of confidence and apprehension as you assume your new role. Be assured, you have also been thoughtfully selected because people in your chain of command are satisfied that in addition to your proven skills, you have the ability to learn. Trust that if you accept the challenge to learn something new every day and put your new knowledge to work, you will acquire the necessary leadership skills to ensure your success.

Dedicate yourself to a study of leadership and to developing a working knowledge of many different leadership styles, employing a variety of skills when guiding your team to greatness. Just like the maestro of an orchestra, you do not need to master every instrument, but you do need to appreciate that each instrument has something unique to contribute to the beauty of the music. Knowing when, where and how to feature your many leadership skills will turn your workgroup into a cohesive orchestra working in close harmony. While some skills must be nurtured over time, others are quick and easy to learn. Here are some essential skills that you can implement today.

## Observe

The first step on your personal path to success as a leader is having a natural curiosity to learn from others, both the good stuff and the bad. Think back to your former jobs and bosses. While some of them were stronger leaders than others, keep in mind that leaders of all stripes and caliber can teach you valuable lessons about what does or does not work. The leadership styles that worked well should be included in the way you guide your team. Things that did not work for a former leader probably will not work for you and should be avoided. Being a keen observer of others will give you a personal point of reference as you learn leadership styles and skills in this book. Here is an example of a lesson learned by observing a productive person who had poor leadership ability.

**Learning Lesson**  At a University based healthcare organization, the long standing leader was a person who had a vision and the latitude to provide resources necessary for developing new and innovative teaching methods.  The promise of professional stimulation drew highly qualified people to the job with the anticipation of developing groundbreaking techniques in education. However, in spite of the professionally stimulating and rewarding work, the team members and lower level leaders suffered under the heavy hand of the leader's narcissism and self-serving agenda.  Even though projects were professionally stimulating, the boss's personality divided the team and created an unbearable work climate.   One by one, exceptionally competent workers left and found employment elsewhere.

**Key point**  Leadership personality sets the tone for the workgroup. Even the most exciting and stimulating work can become intolerable in the wrong environment.  In this case, offering professional growth did not offset the toxic atmosphere created by the leader's personality.

Not all leaders are distant and disconnected.  In successful organizations, there are many stories of creative and empowering leaders setting a positive tone.

**Learning Lesson**  Mary was an outstanding leader known for her ability to connect with her team.  She had a reputation within the organization for always being "one step ahead" with insight into the next problem before her chain of command knew anything was wrong.  The success that Mary achieved was not an accident. She succeeded because her leadership style was based on connecting with each individual beginning on the day they were hired.  An important part of her orientation plan for new team members was a series of feedback sessions.  During orientation Mary created a non-threatening environment and encouraged new people to tell her about anything that did not make sense.  She placed high value on fresh eyes looking at the workflow and feeling safe to speak openly and honestly.  Mary continued the connection process with a town hall meeting for the entire team.  Leveraging her positive relationship with the members, she shared insight gained from the new employee and then listened as the team shared thoughts and solutions. Open communication gave her early warning about potential problems.  By listening to and engaging her team, the group felt a shared responsibility for resolution.   Mary earned recognition as a top leader and her team was recognized as being highly engaged and productive.

**Key point**  As in the first lesson, whether it's by personality or style, the leader sets the tone for the team.  If you consistently listen with good intent, your team members will feel valued and trust is enhanced.

## Seek role models

Expand your search for role models throughout the workplace, into the community and beyond.  As a student of leadership, be discerning about the skills that transform a person into a great leader.  Instead of reflecting on personality and thinking, "Mr. X was a great person," focus on the leadership skills that a 'great person' puts into play.  Visualize two or three strong leaders whom you respect and review the list of positive traits you see.  Let the "whole leader" become a role model for you as you interact with your team. In the future when in doubt, ask, "What would Mr. Y do in this situation?"

Without exception, people who are remembered as great leaders had a vision and were able to engage others in sharing and implementing the vision. For your starter list of role models, spend some research time discovering the leadership styles of the following.

- President John F. Kennedy
    - Introduced the vision: "By the end of the decade we will send a man to the moon and safely return him to earth."
- Dr. Condoleezza Rice
    - As Secretary of state, developed infrastructure for emerging countries to become independent. Required diplomats to be fluent in at least two foreign languages.
- John Wooden
    - Coached UCLA to many undefeated seasons and National Championships but was most known for developing the character of his players.
- Pamela Cipriano
    - Nurse Educator and President of the American Nurses Association has an active voice in developing healthcare policy.
- Michael Dell
    - Re-defined the concept of market innovation by finding ways to put computers in the hands of the greatest number of people at the lowest cost.
- David Robinson
    - Naval Academy graduate and NBA all-star, a proven leader both on and off the court.

Bring your own experiences to life and write down the positive traits of two or three leaders whom you hold in high esteem. Let each person and their traits become characteristics to emulate as you interact with your team. Again, when you're in doubt, ask, "How would Ms. X behave in this situation?"

**Learning Lesson**   Ulysses S. Grant was the commanding general of the Union army in The American Civil War.  In his day, he was a super hero and had he wanted, he could have been carried off the field on the shoulders of his victorious team.  His philosophy was simple: "Find out where your enemy is, get at him as quickly as possible and strike him as hard as possible."  Because of his success commanding the Union army, Grant was elected to be the 18th President of the United States and is viewed by many historians as the worst president in American history.   A great leader in one arena was a failure in another.  In the case of President Grant, the problem was related to having and sharing a vision.  As a president, he didn't have one.  As a war time general, Grant had a clear vision of what needed to be done with an army of men committed to bringing his vision to life.  But, once the war was over and Grant was The President of a peaceful nation, he had no vision.   With no major crisis to attack, he became a "caretaker president" and the easy victim of any scoundrel who could gain an audience with him.  Instead of using the Presidency as the future President Eisenhower did by introducing a new vision of post-war healing, Grant viewed being POTUS as a reward for his military achievements, and history says America suffered.

**Key Point**  The President Grant example serves as a reminder that "the trophies on the shelf will not win today's game."   Keep your vision fresh, share it, promote it and motivate your team to action.

## Find a mentor

*Mentorship is based on "a mutual and sincere desire to elevate one another."*

The ideal mentor is a respected person or friend who has experience with things that you want to learn and master.  Mentoring occurs by mutual consent between two people who are drawn to one another with the common purpose of sharing knowledge and supporting one another.  Frequently, one person has seniority both in position and experience while the other is a neophyte eager to learn from the master.  One of the best ways for you to find a mentor is to establish a network of trusted contacts.  Participate in your network frequently, asking for advice and being available to give the same in return. It is typical to find one or two key people who have a sincere desire to help you solve problems, but be cautious and avoid the mistake of limiting your network to people you see and work with daily.   Expand your network by building friendships and looking for opportunities to connect with others who are not in your immediate area.  Often, someone at a parallel level of responsibility in a different area of the organization, who is experienced and has a reputation for excellence, can become a valuable mentor. As you connect with other leaders, be receptive and allow your personal association to evolve into a mentoring relationship.

**When finding a mentor, consider the following.**

- It's about finding the right person, not finding a person in the right position. Your mentor must have a sincere desire to share knowledge and experience with you and be open to your questions and concerns. Your ideal mentor is an experienced leader who functions at a higher level than yours, and challenges you to improve while giving audience and guidance.
- It is desirable to seek a person who is higher in the chain of command and will encourage you to "up your game." Be careful not to go so high in the chain of command that you end up with a mentor who does not have the time or a sincere interest in developing your career.
- Experienced peers can be effective mentors. Instead of seeking a supervisor as a confidante, you might be well served by finding another frontline leader at a parallel level of responsibility in the organization who has years of experience and is viewed as being highly effective. This person will have faced similar demands and will know how to navigate the channel of challenges that you will most likely encounter.
- A productive mentoring relationship is two-way and must be based on a mutual desire to elevate one another. Even though your mentor may be more experienced, mutual respect opens effective communication. In a great mentoring relationship, both people benefit.

- You do not necessarily need to have a personal friendship with your mentor. The expectation that your guru should also be your best friend may get in the way of the person's sincere desire to help you professionally. Thank your mentor, show your appreciation and always respect the person's personal time and space.

## Expand and grow

Take your leadership skills to a new level by working beyond your comfort zone. An easy but foolish way to appear successful is to limit your activity to areas where you already excel. Hiding within the shell of your current strengths sets a trap that will eventually stifle your growth. In the words of author Sarah Ban Breathnach, "Playing it safe is the riskiest choice that you can ever make." To grow professionally you must resist living in the comfort of the known and build success by seeking new experiences to expand your talent into unknown areas and experience professional growth. Challenge yourself by developing and utilizing a network of trusted colleagues who will help you when you face an unfamiliar task. Have confidence in your ability to learn and view each new task as a personal challenge that will stimulate your professional development. By leaving your comfort zone and becoming more versatile you will better serve your team as well as the larger organization.

**Learning Lesson** Marsha was a well-respected ICU Nurse Manager at a major medical center. One of her primary responsibilities was to staff the ICU 24/7 in a manner that provided safe patient care as well as fairness to those who would be tasked with covering undesirable shifts. In the past, communicating the schedule to the team had not gone smoothly and occasionally people failed to report for scheduled shifts because they were unaware of the assignment. Marsha's supervisor asked her to develop a web-based tool for posting the work schedule and communicating with the team. Marsha had no web development skills and was not comfortable with the assignment. But, in spite of her fear, she readily accepted the challenge and started talking with other leaders in parallel positions to learn about how they solved their communication challenges. Next, she found a person in the IT department to coach her and work with her on the project. By building on the support from her network, Marsha was able to develop a useful and effective web-based tool to post the work schedule and enhance overall communication within the team. Keeping a positive attitude while leveraging her support system, solved the problem and set Marsha up for recognition from her supervisor.

**Key point** Living and working within the comfort zone of what you already do well may create a safe place from which to manage, but it will stifle your growth as a leader. Seek new experiences, accept new responsibilities and tap into your support system to ensure success.

## Keep a Journal

In addition to observing and learning from others, there is great value in learning from your own experience. Set aside time to organize your thoughts and reflect on both the positives and negatives of the day. Writing in the Harvard Business Review,

Nancy Adler emphasizes the importance of journaling as a means to document and learn from your own daily experience. She says, "Gaining access to your own insight isn't difficult; you simply need to commit to reflecting on a daily basis."

To be successful at journaling, you must value the time that is required and block the time on your daily calendar. Use the time to reflect on today and plan for tomorrow. If you are unable to journal at work, schedule a quiet time at home that is dedicated to journaling. Regardless of when or where, make self-reflection an important part of your personal education in leadership.

Journaling may be either hand written in a notebook or documented on your computer. Caution: Journaling on the computer runs the risk of distraction when the journal appears too much like your other work or if email alerts hijack your thoughts. Choose a venue for reflection that has no distractions.

If you are unsure where to start, make a list of several trigger questions and use them to stimulate your thoughts. Use the following questions to get started and then personalize your journal by adding your own TQ's.

Today...

- What was my greatest challenge?
- What affect did my attitude have on the team?
- What leadership skill was most useful?
- Whom could I have asked to help with the most pressing problem?
- What was the most effective thing that I did to support the team?

- Did my actions and decisions support the greater vision and goals?

Set aside time on a weekly basis to review your journal. As you think back over the week, ask these questions.

- Is there a pattern to the challenges that were faced?
- Were a few leadership skills more effective than others?
- Were resources fully utilized?
- Am I satisfied that I did everything to the best of my ability?

Journaling compels you to participate in reviewing your own undeniable experience in a non-threatening and *ce*ntered environment. Daily written reflection "puts the baby to bed" and positions you to grow each day as a leader.

## The Nutshell

Leadership requires the courage of Leo the Lion and the commitment of Mama Bear. Being an effective leader involves totally committing to your team and your organization while making sure that your personal needs are met. Anticipate that your ego will be bumped and bruised along the way but never lose sight of your goal or the talent that you bring to the job. As you begin your journey to becoming a great leader, start today by reviewing and dedicating immediate action on the five skills.

**Be an astute observer.** Leaders, superior and inferior, abound in almost every workplace as well as in your community. Rather than being turned on or off by a personality, be stimulated by behaviors that work. When you exhibit similar behavior, you will probably get similar results so imitate the positive and avoid the negative.

**Seek role models.** Some people barely survive as managers while others develop chemistry with their team and achieve great results. Identify people who elevate others and learn from their example. When seeking role models, look beyond your workplace and organization to find successful people throughout business and industry.

**Find a mentor.** Find that special person in your support network who not only has expertise but also has a sincere desire to coach you to success. Mentoring relationships develop over time and can be priceless. Remember, it's just as rewarding to be a mentor as to have one.

**Expand and grow.** Your comfort zone is safe and secure. Living within your comfort zone gives you a high probability of success on a daily basis, however, it limits your growth and may prevent you from taking the next step up the leadership ladder. Constantly seek to expand your skills and then use your support network to guide you through the new challenge.

**Keep a journal.** By taking time to review and document the day's activities, you will get a clear picture of things that could have been done differently. Learning from your own real life experience raises your awareness and sets you up to better handle similar situations the next time they arise.

*Leader Reader 1, Authentic Lessons in Leadership* offers you a multitude of tools to be an outstanding leader. Be passionate about leadership, dedicate yourself to learning something new every day, and have confidence that using these tools will turn your dream of leadership into a story of success.  Your bosses selected you as a leader for a multitude of good reasons and they are confident in your ability to lead.  Can you do it?  Yes, you can!

*"Knowledge is a good thing but only has value when it's put to good use."*

# Chapter 2

# The Foundation for Trust

## Personality Matters, Character Counts

Your basic outlook on life determines how you think and feel which, in turn, affects your behavior. Are you optimistic, outgoing, or perhaps cautious and introspective? Personality affects how your team members interact with you and with one another. The attitude and behavior you exude exposes your character and because you're the leader, your character counts.

- **Personality:** A set of distinctive traits that is the sum of the person's behavioral and emotional makeup.
- **Character:** The essential nature of ethical thoughts and actions that distinguishes the individual.

Psychologists confirm that we are born with basic personality traits and though we cannot alter our inherent persona, we can control how we develop and display it. Timid people can learn to be great public speakers and extroverts can learn to tone it down. Your team is constantly observing you, and they will respond more positively to a leader whose personality is warm and inclusive than they will to a leader who is distant and authoritarian. Whether you are naturally timid, outgoing, passive or assertive, leverage your strengths and strengthen your shortcomings as you develop new dimensions to your personality.

Anyone who has had more than one job has had more than one boss and is in a position to make comparisons. Employees quickly grow to like or dislike a boss and they often base their opinions on the character of the leader. In workplace engagement surveys that connect leadership style with employee satisfaction these are two common conclusions. 1) Leaders with a focus on displaying ethical character and building a trusting work environment get high marks. 2) Truthfulness, transparency and the ability to affirm others are linked to high employee satisfaction scores. Clearly, personality and character do count.

By using the following concepts in an honest and constructive self-assessment, you can raise awareness of your personality strengths and the areas in which you can improve. These concepts will also put you in touch with your depth of character.

## Character and Personality

The combination of ethical behavior in achieving a goal, and being sensitive to the needs of the individual team members, is an important dimension of successful leadership. Who you are and what you do matters to your team. By being simultaneously ethical and sensitive, you establish a working climate in which team members interact well with one another, and with you. Here is an example.

*"Be more concerned with your character than your reputation, because your character is what you really*

*are, while your reputation is merely what others think you are."* John Wooden

The late great UCLA basketball coach, John Wooden, won 10 national championships in 12 years, including an unprecedented four undefeated seasons during his tenure. Coach Wooden focused on a goal and he role-modeled desired behavior while encouraging personal greatness in each member of the team. "What you are as a person is far more important than what you are as a basketball player….never curse, never criticize a teammate," was his code of conduct, and to prove his sincerity, Wooden the leader always released the team from practice on time, every time. Coach Wooden taught the team that when each player used his best self, he could play the game to the best of his ability and success would follow. The focus was on personal excellence on and off the court and had little to do with the score on the board.

The integrity of Coach Wooden created a foundation of trust within the team where each person sincerely wanted to help team mates perform at a higher level. This kind of role modeling is equally essential for you as a healthcare leader.

## Ethical Qualities

There are four ethical qualities that define you as a leader and promote a cohesive, winning team. The qualities of *integrity, honesty, transparency* and *fairness* are foundational building blocks for creating trust. They all overlap in some way but are clearly or subtly distinctive in others. In the end, your personality will infuse them with life. Coach Wooden lived to be ninety-nine years old and that is a long time to have to look in the mirror and live with your legacy.

## 1. Integrity

### *"Reputation is who others think you are. Integrity is who you really are."*

Integrity is the inner moral compass that guides you and demands that you adhere strictly to moral and ethical principles. Integrity is *who you are*. Having integrity is demonstrated by aligning your words, your values and your vision with your behavior. With integrity, walking the walk is more important than maintaining the peace. The leader with integrity has the courage to speak up when other's actions do not align with the promises they have made.

Not all leaders have a moral compass. In 2016 the news media exposed the lack of integrity in a number of bank executives at Wells Fargo Bank. While promising fiduciary responsibility to the bank's customers and shareholders alike, the bank engaged in illegal activities that led to the creation of millions of bogus accounts complete with fees that were passed along to unsuspecting account holders. Plainly, the behavior of the leaders did not align with the values they professed to their clientele. In the end, Wells Fargo was required to pay large fines with restitution to customers. Lack of executive integrity caused a loss in stock value and, more importantly, in consumer confidence.

It is easy to be inspired by stories of integrity in some people, or to be offended by the lack of integrity in others, while ignoring one's own behavior. Leaders are given opportunities on a daily basis to set the tone in the workplace by demonstrating integrity in our actions and to do so consistently. Working in a trusting environment, encourages self-disclosure of mistakes and allows us to point out lapses in others without threatening their self-esteem. In contrast, a threatening work environment in which every mistake is punished has the opposite effect. You can only lead to the extent that others are willing to follow, and if you want them to follow your lead, you must establish predictability by leading with integrity.

In leadership, there are two common threats to your integrity to avoid.

**Loss of focus.** Keeping a focus on your team and your own behavior is essential for promoting integrity. Busy leaders frequently feel the pressure of large volumes of work combined with short timelines, and the pressure to meet a deadline or complete a project can distract you from promises that you made to your team. Your ability to lead is diminished when you focus more intensely on administrative tasks and less on the needs of your team. Remaining focused on the team while consistently role modeling desired behavior reinforces your personal integrity.

**Failure to follow through** on agreements and commitments separates your words from your actions and represents a lack of integrity. Words and actions must go hand in hand. Frontline leaders often agree to things before they have a clear understanding of what is being requested. But, a leader must be thoughtful when making commitments because when you promise an action, your team expects results. Later, after additional information becomes available, your initial *yes* response may need to be changed to *maybe* or even to *no*. If yes turns to no without an explanation, your integrity is compromised, and if *yes* hangs in space without follow-up, it will be viewed as an empty promise. Avoid the knee jerk affirmative that is meant to appease a team member. Rather than giving a quick nod, ask for more information to clarify the request. You are the leader. It's okay to say *no* if you are not certain that you can follow-up with the request. But if you say, "Yes," follow through.

## 2. Honesty

> ***"Always tell the truth. That way you don't have to remember what you said."*** — **Mark Twain, author**

Honesty is characterized by truthfulness, sincerity and frankness in all matters and is essential for creating a trusting environment. It is tied to the perception of fairness and is deeply engrained into our mindset starting at a very early age. When children were small, most parents spent time and effort teaching their children the concept that honesty is the best policy. In school, youngsters were taught to imitate George Washington and Abe Lincoln, two good leaders with reputations for being truthful.

But, after those same children grew up, it became apparent to them that though they may have been taught the value of veracity, they may not always hear "whole truth" in the real world. They may not be expected to tell the whole truth. They have learned that people lie. Watching today's public figures, Facebook friends, news outlets, and co-workers alternate between stretching and hiding the truth, or just plain lying, causes us to question the values we were taught. In your leadership, shades of the truth will have a polarizing effect and down the road there will be consequences. Politicians who get caught lying lose elections; news outlets who publish mere versions of the truth lose circulation; dishonest celebrities lose their fans; and business people who lead with lies get fired. Being less than truthful is a short-term fix that does not work for others, and it will not work for you. All successful leaders intrinsically place a high value on absolute honesty. Be sincere with your team to promote communication, connectedness and security.

Colon Powell, retired Secretary of State and former Chairman of the Joint Chiefs of Staff, established a reputation for absolute honesty both in his military career and during his term as Secretary of State. Within the military community, Powell's personal rules were well known and included, "Avoid having your ego so close to your position that when your position falls, so does your ego." Powell believed that personal honesty in all matters should be apparent through the things that you say and do. His commitment to truthfulness earned him high praise in his role with the US Military and the Joint Chiefs of Staff. In the 2016 Presidential election campaign the issue of using a personal server for email was the subject an emotional and legal debate between the two major political parties. Although Powell could have remained silent, he came forward and volunteered the information that many years earlier - in the infancy of email - he had used a private server while fulfilling the role of Secretary of State. Powell was not as much concerned about the outcome of the election as being true to his commitment to absolute honesty.

Successful frontline leaders place a high value on absolute honesty and in your leadership role you will learn that the adults who raised you were right. Honesty is not just the best policy, it is the only policy.

## *"To be respected, you must be both honest and forthright."*

Being honest is more than just refraining from telling a lie.  Honesty includes the dimension of being forthright by revealing the entire truth.  Ask any teen's parents and they will tell you of times when they made a decision based on the story they were told, only to find out later that several important details were left out.  The teen may have been perfectly honest in what he said, but, by intentionally withholding details, what was unsaid turned the story into a lie.

Being honest is more than just refraining from telling a lie. Remember, honesty has the dimension of being forthright by revealing the entire truth. Shrouding the truth in a veil of partial honesty can and does occur in healthcare and can directly affect patient safety.  Zero medication errors is the standard taught to nurses but despite the careful vial-reading procedures put in place by the department, mistakes do occur.  Years ago, I was working with an anesthesia student who administered a long acting muscle relaxant by mistake when a shorter acting drug was supposed to have been given.  The student knew at the time that he had given the patient wrong drug but he felt that because he had administered a relaxant, it didn't matter.  As the instructor I spent an hour trying to determine why the drug was not performing as expected.  Had the student been forthright and identified the mistake, the team could have dealt with it quickly, however, not having the full truth triggered us to believe that something was wrong with the patient.

Half-truths related to administrative issues can also waste valuable time and have the long-lasting consequence of destroying trust.  In one of my leadership positions I had the opportunity to mentor several up-and-comers who were given the opportunity to manage projects.  In one case, a team member in charge of a project was instructed to check in with me at intervals and with the team to review his progress and to receive permission before taking the project to the next level.   When I requested an update, the person responded that the project was "going well."  Shortly after receiving the actual report, I learned that the project had been taken to completion including signing of a contract for services.  Even though the person did a nice job on the project and said truthfully that it was progressing, the lack of forthright communication caused me to lose trust and to find someone else for the next project.

As a leader, you must establish the benchmark of behavior that you expect from your team.  When anyone on the team tells a partial truth or withholds important information, it is perceived by others as a lie and your ability to make appropriate leadership decisions will be compromised.  For example, consider the problems that Beth encountered by withholding information.

**Beth's Story**   A new Nurse Manager Leader, Beth was in charge of 62 Nurses and Technicians.  She wanted to be successful and gain a reputation for being the best leader in the building.  She believed that people work best when they are happy so she frequently shielded her workgroup from bad news or policy changes that might have a negative impact on morale.  Her fear was that by sharing too much information, the team would resist and become passive-aggressive.  She wanted to be popular and still have her team be productive.  Although she never told a lie to any member of the group, she withheld the whole truth on more than one occasion.  Her lack of forthrightness culminated toward the end of the first year when the team learned about an unpopular policy change through rumor and gossip rather than from Beth.   The team finally realized that they could not trust their leader to openly share the truth and morale suffered. Requests for transfer to another area of the hospital became frequent and recruiting was difficult. In order to restore team morale and engagement, Beth was replaced.

## Yes means yes

Following through with commitments is not only proof of your integrity, it is another platform for demonstrating honesty to your team. Always follow up and do exactly what you say you will do and attach a timeline to commitments to ensure completion. Allowing your team to have expectations that turn out to be empty promises is like being partially honest, and when crystal clear follow-up is absent, morale suffers and your lack of integrity is exposed. Jason's leadership started differently than Beth's.

**Jason's Story** Jason was promoted to his position as Nurse Manager of a Surgical ICU based on his exceptional skill and knowledge as a frontline Nurse. Jason was a high achiever who consistently volunteered for the most difficult cases and became an expert at providing hands-on patient care. He could work at laser pace, creating a blur as he moved back and forth caring for two challenging patients simultaneously. Jason earned his reputation for excellence from being self-sufficient. Jason's workload increased when he became the leader, but, rather than allowing others to slow his work, he accepted very little help, and continued to focus instead on the work at hand. In his new role, Jason worked with the same intensity when addressing administrative duties. He made very little time to listen to people and when he was cornered with a request, Jason quickly said, "Yes," moving post-haste on to the next task. The team learned that his rapid-fire responses seldom led to action.  As you would guess, the team felt betrayed and disconnected from their leader because of the lack of follow through.  Although Jason worked hard, the team members sensed that their concerns weren't important enough to be heard.  Quickly, Jason acquired a reputation for being aloof and self-absorbed which translated as dishonesty. Like Beth, Jason was replaced.

## The value of no

One of the most powerful and honest words that you can use is a simple "no."  Leaders are expected to "make it work," to do more and more, often with less and less, to have happy and engaged team members, and to say, "Yes!" to everything.  Having a positive attitude is certainly important but the overuse of yes will lead to over-committing yourself, or your team, and may make it difficult to fulfill promises.   There are times and places where a simple no can actually be used to your advantage and contribute to a positive outcome.  Here are some thoughts on how to make a positive out of the negative.

- When aligning your time and resources, sometimes a better outcome is created by saying no.
- *No* can help restore control in a chaotic situation.
- Allowing or encouraging others to say *no* gives them a sense of control and will lead to a better result when you are negotiating.
- Saying *no* enables you to slow the process and gain additional information.

## Honesty in communication

Virtue in what you do isn't quite enough by itself. Your team looks to you and your leadership with the expectation that what you say and what you do as you interact with them will be honest and forthright, including the way in which you communicate. Open and honest communication keeps you connected with each individual on the team. When they assess your level of honesty as a leader, your team will rate you on the following:

- Your ability to share both good and bad news
- Your willingness to listen and use ideas generated by the team when problem solving
- Your commitment to timely follow-through on promises you have made

Beth and Jason are both good people with good intentions, however, they failed to communicate honestly and effectively with their teams and both became unsuccessful leaders. To be a successful leader, embrace the clear personal mandate that you must combine honesty with accountability in order to build a climate of trust within the workgroup.

***You can't lead without the trust of your workgroup, and they won't trust you if you are not honest***

## 3. Transparency

Transparency is clarity and authenticity in all of your interactions with others. To be really effective, it is two-way. Your team shares your desire for the opportunity to excel and when you collaborate in an open and cohesive relationship with your team, you encourage high performance. By working in a team situation where two-way transparency is the established modus operandi, further trust is built and you will all have a chance for exceptional performance.

Integrity and honesty have both been identified as essential characteristics for effective leadership. The concept of transparency builds on honesty by taking it to the next level, disclosing not only the truth but the evidence behind the truth. Rather than simply reporting the bottom line on the department budget, you can be transparent by opening the books so that there is an opportunity to review where each dollar was spent. You can enhance your transparency as a leader when you say that vacation time is not available if you back it up by letting the team review the schedule and see for themselves that the maximum number of people are already scheduled to be away.

To gain a reputation for being a transparent leader, you must first be truthful and then share the evidence that supports your statements. By sharing openly, both the good and the bad, your team will reciprocate and trust is further built.

**Transparent leadership is evidenced by…**

- Giving a message that remains the same regardless of who is listening
- Sharing the background behind the truth
- Keeping commitments
- Owning your own mistakes without blaming others
- Welcoming feedback from others

Watch out for the transparency trap of acting like a politician who overwhelms the team with a "data dump," in which the team receives so much information that they can't possibly make sense of it. When using transparency to build trust, you must not only provide information but it must be in a format that is accurate and easy to understand.

### *To encourage transparency, it must be OK not to be OK.*

The greatest block to transparency is fear. In healthcare, we are taught that patient's lives are at risk therefore perfection is expected. We may fear that being fully transparent and self-reporting weaknesses or errors threatens our image of perfection. The fear of imperfection is just one more barrier to full transparency created by a leader or team member. It takes courage to self-report and to build an environment where it's okay to be imperfect. As leaders, open the door to transparency by having a willingness to share all information that can be shared and having the courage to admit your own mistakes. If you openly promote honesty that is transparent, you will generate the attitude that regardless of the challenge, "We can work together to achieve the goal." Role-model desired behavior to your team and let them see that transparency opens the door to growth. In a trusting environment, two-way transparency about your challenges will stimulate your team to step up and help you find solutions.

### Transparency tips

- **Disclosure should be factual.** When possible, make sure that your team has full access to all of the information regarding a policy or a problem. Eventually the team will learn the full truth and if it differs from what you told them, your credibility will vanish.  When your commitment to transparency is violated, information that you provide the group will be scrutinized and the team will have difficulty taking you at your word.   If you have facts that can't yet be disclosed, let the team know your limitation.  Assure them that they will have all the facts as soon as possible.  It's transparent to tell the team that an issue remains under discussion and that you have been asked not to discuss details.

- **Clarity removes confusion.** Leaders are busy people who are frequently called upon to multitask in a chaotic environment.  When in a rush and focused on a deadline, it is easy to speak in general terms and omit the details.  The team may all agree that the goal is to score a touchdown, however, there's no TD unless they know which play to run.  Providing clear information to your group is essential in achieving the goal.   Written criteria for assessing progress will clarify expectations and give direction to the project.
- **Shortcomings are opportunities.** You and each of your team members have personal weaknesses and from time to time you all may make mistakes.  When that happens, don't envelop personal shortcomings in half-truths for fear of exposure.  Explain yourself in an optimistic tone with the expectation of finding a solution and encourage team members to do the same.  Use transparency to convert a personal lapse into an opportunity for growth.

Adding transparency to the building blocks of integrity and honesty establishes a solid foundation to build upon as a leader.   Here are some of the advantages of leading with transparency.

- **Transparency fosters authenticity.** Greatness is achieved through teamwork and teams work best when each individual knows and respects their team mates.  Your candor with each member of the team affords them the opportunity to appreciate your personal values.  In return, you gain insight into theirs.
- **Problems are solved faster.**   When errors are punished and error-makers are publicly humiliated, there is zero incentive for transparency.  When errors are hidden, time and effort is wasted looking for the source of a problem.  In a work culture where an error is a learning opportunity, the group will identify and solve problems more quickly and effectively.  Transparency removes the element of surprise and offers your team the freedom to support one another without questioning motives.
- **Transparency builds security.** Your group wants you to be the perfect all-star leader, but, they also want you to be human.  Being fully transparent about your personal challenges and concerns – not your personal life - builds security within the group and makes them feel safe to share equally with you.  As a leader, you will be amazed at how many people will step up to a challenge once they feel safe.
- **Engagement is enhanced.** Engagement is a term used by managers to describe the employee who understands the greater goal and is "all in" with a commitment to achieve success.  Nothing kills engagement more quickly than a lack of transparency.  If you want your group to be fully engaged, you must provide them with as much information as possible in a format that is clear. Never underestimate or lack appreciation for the talent that your team brings to the workplace.

## 4. Fairness

As with honesty, we were taught fairness in childhood when adults expected us to treat others the way we wanted to be treated. We teach our children to share their toys with another person as we quip, "Sharing is caring." We don't throw the bat at the ump over a bad call and we don't hide behind the office door when we're not really busy. If we make an effort to show others how to play fair, we affirm the expectation of being treated fairly. Giving and receiving fairness is a learned skill that extends beyond the teen years into adulthood. As competent adults, your team expects fair treatment from you and from the institution. If this expectation of fairness is not met, the reactions of group members may range from silence, to passive/aggressive behavior to open rebellion. None of these outcomes bode well for you as a leader and ultimately, the entire group will falter, maybe even fail.

My personal experience as a leader is that people are willing, even happy to assume a difficult or undesirable task if they perceive that others are doing their fair share. Leaders create the perception of favoritism if they make preferential assignments in order to avoid pushback from difficult team members. The perception or the reality of unfairness will always cause the morale and engagement of an entire group to suffer. Wilma Gillis, the longstanding Chief CRNA at the University of Wisconsin, says that the key to success as a leader is to "...develop a system that is fair to all, known by all and enforced equally within the group." Current literature related to team leadership in business and industry confirms Wilma's assessment.

Leaders set the tone in the workplace and the way in which you enforce and apply the rules will determine whether or not your team perceives fairness.  If their perception is that you are fair and care about them, they will double down and fight to support you and the success of the group.  On the other hand, if their perception is one of unfairness, when you stumble, they will stand back and watch you fall.  The bottom line is that fairness is an essential element for a successful frontline leader.

Absolute fairness in the workplace, along with honesty and transparency, encourages collaboration.  In contrast, when fairness depends on the situation, your team will quickly divide into cliques competing with one another.  To be viewed as fair, you must clearly define the expectations and you must enforce the rules in all situations.  Exhibit authentic leadership by moving fairness in the workplace from lip service to concrete reality, keeping the following in mind.

**Fairness in scheduling.**  People enter the field of healthcare for many reasons, not the least of which is the sincere desire to help others and make a difference in their lives.  Throughout training, we are taught to make sacrifices to ensure that our patients receive exceptional care.  New employees are eager to take undesirable shifts thinking that they are filling an important need.  Once on the job, newbies quickly learn that some assignments are better than others and that some shifts are not convenient to their lifestyle.  Things are only fair or unfair in the context of comparison to how others are treated.   Working two weeks of night shift plus two weekends every month may seem fair and reasonable until you discover that you are the only person in the workgroup required to cover that many undesirable shifts.  Leaders are resource managers and your most valuable resource is your workgroup.   To preserve the integrity of the group, ensure that each individual has the same opportunity for reward and the same obligation to cover difficult assignments or undesirable shifts.

**All members must be heard equally.** To promote fairness, you must have a collaborative one-on-one relationship with each member of your team. Getting to know people beyond the credentials they presented when they were hired and the job description that they are expected to follow, involves connecting with and learning about what motivates each person. Every individual on the team must know that they can talk openly with you, that you will listen, and that though you may not be able to grant every request, you will hear each person equally. No single voice will be heard above the other. What may seem to be a small issue to you is important to the person bringing it to your attention. Listening carefully, taking action when you can, and being sympathetic when you are unable to help are behaviors that promote the sense of fairness.

**Promotions and bonuses must be transparent.** A fair, open and transparent bonus system will stimulate people to achieve at a higher level. There is no quicker way to undermine the morale of the group than to give promotions and perks to a selected few while leaving the rest of the group to do the hard work without recognition. Clearly identifying the criteria used for determining promotion and bonus sets realistic expectations and creates the platform for fair and equal treatment of each person under your supervision. For some, being recognized as one the highest level of achievers is more important than the actual bonus money received. Here is an example.

A group of Nurse Anesthetists in a large Anesthesiology department had a pay/benefit system that included an annual bonus. The system gave each member of the group the same bonus at the end of the year regardless of their contribution.  The most engaged and the hardest working in the group received the same reward as those who were nowhere to be found when extra work popped up, creating a sense of unfairness among the most productive members.   Based on feedback from the team, leadership moved to a new rewards program that recognized and rewarded the high achievers.  A three-tiered bonus system that gave a larger bonus to those who consistently performed at a higher level was developed with the intent to incentivize desired behavior.  Criteria were developed that gave every member of the team the same opportunity to earn the highest bonus.  After the criteria were established, it was made transparent to the group so that every team member knew the requirements for earning each level of bonus.  Half-way through the year the bonus rules were reviewed with the group as a reminder of expectations.  At the end of the year, performance was reviewed and bonuses were given at all three levels with the large majority of the group earning at mid-level. The open and transparent bonus system was a success and fairness prevailed.  Being openly fair and equal, the policy generated enthusiasm within the group to work harder and to contribute more knowing everyone had equal opportunity for recognition.  Fairness works!

**All group members must have an appeal process.**  A person's perception of fairness is his reality.  Regardless of your sincere intention to be a fair leader to each member of the group, at some point a member of the group will feel that they have been treated unfairly.  Your response to the grievance from an individual team member will send a message to the entire team regarding your view of fairness.  If you do not respond quickly and with a sense of equality, the entire team will be affected.   The team trusts that you will be just and they will feel betrayed if a grievance is not addressed.

Even though you may think you're being even-handed, some team members may perceive it differently. If they think something is not equitable, they will bring the problem to you. Avoid being evasive or dismissive and reach a resolution by using the following steps to address grievances.

- **Step 1: Acknowledge and affirm.** When a person has a grievance, acknowledge and affirm that they have the right to their perception. If left unresolved, the unhappiness of an individual can grow like a cancer and consume the morale of the entire group. By welcoming the complaint and listening to both the facts and the emotion behind the grievance, you will gain valuable information. Listening to one person's complaint may reveal a larger issue that needs to be resolved. You do not have to agree with the premise of the grievance, however, you must accept their perception of unfairness and use that information as a starting point to move forward. Be sincere when you thank the person for bringing the problem to your attention. Schedule a future date to meet again if it will be necessary. Often, a complaint arises from poor communication and all that is needed for resolution is to share information.
- **Step 2: Listen with good intent.** Listen to understand. Restate the concerns of the other person and do not move forward until you can re-state the person's concern to their satisfaction. A sincere desire to understand from the other person's viewpoint reinforces the perception of fairness.
- **Step 3: Gather information.** Things are never as they appear on the surface. It is likely that there is more to the

problem than either of you know at your first meeting. Commonly, things are not as bad as claimed by the person with the grievance nor as good as hoped by the leader. By gathering information, both sides become aware of the reasoning behind the other person's position. As with communication, the gathering and sharing of information may be all it takes to clarify a misunderstanding and resolve the conflict.

- **Step 4: Set a timeline resolution.** I once worked for a leader who appeared to listen to the concerns of each team member, however, issues were never resolved. The team quickly became aware that our leader "listened intently and heard nothing." Good faith listening is great only when it leads to resolution. "I'll follow-up next week," is not enough. Establish a written timeline and adhere to it.
- **Step 5: Bring to closure.** Having a venue to voice disagreement or appeal a decision is only effective if mutual agreement on the solution is reached. Schedule a final meeting for both parties to agree on factual accuracy, then work with the person(s) to identify points of agreement and to develop solution strategy. Remember that disagreements have an emotional component and offering the person a sincere thank you for their input and point of view are in order. When the meeting is over, both of you need to keep the commitments you made and bring the issue and solution to closure.

## Building Trust

> *"Trust is built by many small things over time, and it can be ruined in a single encounter."*

Trust is an outgrowth of the four ethical components of integrity, honesty, transparency and fairness, and is essential for a workgroup to be actively engaged and to work at their full potential. Put differently, it is not possible to build an effective workgroup without having a trusting environment. With an ethical foundation solidly in place, a focus on building trust within the team is the next step toward excellence.

In preparation for writing *Leader Reader 1*, I did interviews and had discussions with multiple healthcare leaders. Without exception, they all agree that two-way trust between the leader and the group is a critical factor in effective leadership. These quotes from famous people reinforce the importance of trust within your team:

- "The glue that holds all relationships together - including the relationship between the leader and the followers - is trust, and trust is based on integrity." - *Brian Tracy, CEO Brian Tracy Int'l*
- "We need people in our lives with whom we can be as open as possible. To have real conversations with people may seem like such a simple, obvious suggestion, but it involves courage and risk." - *Thomas Moore, Irish Poet*
- "Trust is like blood pressure. It's silent, vital to good health, and if abused it can be deadly." - *Frank Sonnenberg, Author*

Looking beyond the healthcare workplace, trust has emerged as a major issue in our society. Over the past three decades, trust in the

Federal Government has taken a nose dive and now is at an all-time low. In the same insecure environment, parents are pulling their children from public schools because they do not trust the quality of education. Opinion polls indicate that majority of Americans do not trust the authenticity of the information being aired by network news. In many workplaces, trust is lost as employers change benefits packages, consolidate jobs or restructure entire businesses, thus delivering less than promised when workers were hired. The growing distrust of authority in general can easily be transferred not only to the workplace, but just as easily to you, the leader. It is challenging for you to build trust in a team of skeptics. Despite the challenge, make a commitment to establishing a workplace where trust is foundational. Displaying ethical qualities and connecting one on one with each team member is the first step in building lasting trust.

Leaders are responsible for defining policy, procedures and workflow while expecting compliance from the team. Although the team may comply because of the authority of your position, be very careful not to confuse compliance with trust. Workers will obey your commands, but, whether they embrace your directives, or give reluctant compliance, depends upon the level of trust that you have developed with them.

Building trust is like building a tower; it can only be built to a height that is supported by the foundation. My experience as a leader is that using the four ethical qualities discussed in this chapter will enable you to build a tower of trust in your workplace and with your team. Although all four ethical qualities are important, integrity is the foundation that supports the structure.

Integrity is within you. It is the moral compass that identifies who you are. Dictated by and melded with your distinctive personality, your moral center defines how you conduct your business and relate to your team. Below are examples of ways that you can use your moral compass to build trust and to set an example that others will want to follow.

## Build Trust with Integrity

- Show confidence in yourself and your team. Your team members want a leader who is decisive and has a confident attitude. They want the comfort of sensing that you understand the big picture and are able to protect their needs while achieving the organization's goals. Leading with integrity means that you know and you do what is right for the team. Likewise, your team is made of competent professionals and they deserve to know that you respect and appreciate their sense of ethics. You demonstrate integrity not only when you hold true to your values, but also when you recognize the value that others add to the group.
- **Keep confidentiality.** Because effective communication is a two-way process, as you earn the trust of your workgroup, you will become privy to more and more information of a personal nature. Team members share personal information with you because they feel safe and sense that you have the integrity to protect their wellbeing. The ability to keep confidentiality is foundational to a trusting relationship. If people feel that they will be betrayed, they will not open up to you nor will they be fully receptive to the things you share with them. Violating your principles by not keeping confidentiality will kill communication between you and your workgroup.

- **Take issues directly to the person concerned.** My careers in both military and civilian jobs have consistently affirmed that a leader with integrity addresses issues directly with the person involved. A weak leader addresses the entire group for the sins of the individual by saying, "Some people are not in compliance with the policy." In essence the entire group is reprimanded because the leader does not have the fortitude to address the individual. Obviously, trust is never two-way with a flimsy leader who can't confront individuals, nor can group trust be built.

## Build Trust with Honesty

Once a solid foundation of integrity has been established, trust can be elevated with honesty. Being truthful in all interactions with your team and with your chain of command is essential. Being honest most of the time, part of the time, or partly honest all of the time is not good enough because a single lapse can cause trust to crumble. Below are examples of ways in which you can use honesty to enhance trust within your team.

- **Clarify expectations.** The first step in managing expectations is to honestly and openly communicate your expectations to the group. Members of the group may have false expectations when your vision and goals are not clearly defined and communicated. Let the group know what you need and why it is important. Do not view pushback as resistance but as an indicator that clarification is needed.
- **Speak with good purpose.** When communicating with your workgroup, you may not always have good news to deliver. Here is a secret. The people in your workgroup already

know that the news won't always be good and they are stronger than you think.  They accept that problems arise and will want to help resolve them.  Use asset based words to focus on the many positives while recognizing the negatives and seek ways to enhance the positive. Speak with good intent and have confidence in your team.  When they feel your desire to be truthful while looking out for the best interest of the group, they will back you even when you deliver bad news.

- **Encourage honest and open feedback.** Your team has expectations that may or may not be similar to yours.  Because trust must be two-way, encourage open dialogue where team members can openly share their expectations of you as a supervisor and of the institution.  Being receptive in a non-critical manner tells each team member that they are valued and their opinion counts.
- **Be sincere in your reactions.**  Honesty is more than what you say; it also involves how you say it.  When you speak to your group, the actual content you deliver is only part of the equation.  Your tone of voice and body language send a stronger message than your words. Your tone and body language are often louder than your words so be aware of how you are being perceived when you interact with your team members.  Bland smiling or deep-furrowed brows are equally negative in opposite ways. If your words say one thing but your tone and body language send a different message, trust will erode.  Display a sincere desire for two-way truth.

## Build Trust with Transparency

After establishing absolute integrity and honesty, you can interweave transparency.  Transparency adds the elements of clarity and authenticity which broaden honesty and elevate trust.  Remember, transparency builds upon honesty by revealing the data behind the truth.  Here are some ways to add transparency to your leadership approach.

- **Leverage the benefit of transparency.** It's easy to get team support for new initiatives when the group feels that they are part of the solution and essential to the success of the project.   They can only feel connected if they are informed.  Quickly reveal all that is allowed to be shared to multiply the benefits of being open.   Assure the group that their support is essential and that they will be told as much as possible as soon as possible.
- **Openly publish pay/benefits information.**  This is both fair and transparent. Telling a worker that they are being treated fairly has no meaning unless they can see the data to support the statement.  The pay scale and benefits package must be published and available for all to see.  Relate the process that was used in developing a benefits package that represents fair market value.  In addition, if a bonus structure is in place, the criteria must be published and available for each team member to review.
- **Make data meaningful.**  Politicians have a talent for overwhelming us with meaningless information.  As the team leader, you must extract the data that affects your team and has the most impact, and present it in a format that is easily understood.  By working in good faith to distill the important pieces of information and sharing them honestly with your team, trust is developed.

## Build Trust with Fairness

With three building blocks in place, you are ready to top it with the ethical quality of fairness. You have team members with amazing talent who want to make a difference for the patients and for the organization. They willingly sacrifice to ensure that patients receive the highest possible quality of care. They need to be able to assume that others on the team are making equal sacrifices. To promote fairness within the team, consider the following.

- **Establish boundaries.** People of all ages, all levels of education and all backgrounds are always exploring the boundaries. Adults often express thankfulness for the boundaries that they did not appreciate as children. Likewise, your team looks to you to set boundaries as a means of leveling the playing field and establishing fairness. When you explain the purpose of the rules and you enforce them uniformly, your workgroup is comforted by the transparency and the fairness.
- **Raise the bar on performance.** Healthcare teams are constantly seeking ways to use evidence based data to improve patient outcomes. You and your team are vital to that effort and often the frontline healthcare workers are the ones carrying out new protocols. Regardless of who developed the protocol, those who implement it are vital to the process and fairness is enhanced when they are recognized for their contribution.
- **Emphasize appreciation.** Throughout both the healthcare and business communities, highly desirable workplaces have leaders who recognize and appreciate the talents of each

individual on the team.  A leader who is connected to the team observes motivated people doing exceptional work on a daily basis.  Take time to recognize and thank them.  Set up a format for weekly or monthly recognition of achievements.  By showcasing the talent of your team you create a sense of fairness and the knowledge that they will be recognized for their work.  Fairness fosters trust.

Developing trust takes time and a commitment to establishing an honest relationship with each individual team member. Leaders are in charge of defining workplace policy and because of the authority of your position, the team will comply.  But, don't confuse compliance with trust.   Although the team will obey your directives, whether your team embraces your directives, or gives reluctant compliance depends upon the level of trust that you have developed with them.

## The Nutshell

Whether you are new or experienced in leadership, you are likely reading this book because you want to be a better leader, hopefully a great one.  In addition, it's appropriate to want personal success while building a team that can be recognized for excellence.  Regardless of the job you were trained to do, if you are a leader who wants your team to be successful in every way, you will use the foundation of integrity and the building blocks of honesty, transparency and fairness to build trust in your leadership.

You must not only use these qualities but they must be apparent in the way you use your personality to give them life.  That's your job as the leader, that's your challenge.

The concept of using building blocks is simple to visualize, but it's not quite as easy to see how they overlap and connect. With curiosity and a focused approach to learning about leadership, using the ethical qualities will become not only manageable, but they will become authentic leadership behavior. Communicating with the less than forthright worker, coping with the narcissistic boss, making yourself heard to a poor listener, meeting last-minute deadlines, evaluating team members fairly are no longer larger than life issues when your integrity is well-founded and deeply grounded. Your job as the leader is to keep your eye on the vision and to use character and personality to help your group grow, a goal that is most easily accomplished by building trust.

If some of the traits associated with successful leadership do not describe you, don't be discouraged. Have confidence in your natural talents and your ability to learn. Use self-evaluation as the educational tool that reminds you that you're both human and normal, that education and training enabled you to be successful in your profession. And success in your profession placed you in the position that attracted you to leadership. The same commitment to continuing your education and training will propel you to leadership excellence.

***The authentic leader walks away at the end of the day and smiles, knowing that everyone on the team feels important to the process.***

# Chapter 3

# The Path to Leadership

Selecting a new leader is an important and yet commonly overlooked opportunity to build a team that supports the greater mission and vision of the organization. Organizations of all sizes depend upon skilled leadership to meet those goals and the expectations of all the stake holders. To provide superb and satisfying care for the patients by a superb and satisfied staff, they are constantly seeking talented people to assume skilled leadership roles. Those tasked with hiring and developing highly effective leaders are consistently asking, "Where can we find effective leaders?"

There are many paths to leadership and all of them are viable. Every leader has taken a unique path to their current position or to the one they are seeking, and most likely each has had an interesting journey. The memories and experiences along the way shape the leadership style that the leader brings to the job. Writing in *Psychology Today*, Peter Noel Murray PhD affirms the importance of memories and notes that memories are often different from actual experience. He says that we base our decisions on "memories more than actual experience." By knowing your path to leadership and the origin of your memories, you can gain insight into your decision-making and ultimately, your leadership behavior.

Rather than allowing your past experience to control who you are, developing creative approaches to team building and problem solving by building on your memories is an authentic leadership opportunity.

## Born Leaders

A born leader is one who has an engaging personality and an inborn aptitude for influencing others. All teachers at any level of education can name one or two students in every class who are people magnets. Their peers see them as dominant personalities, high-energy, natural leaders inherently gifted in guiding others in either positive or negative ways. Due to their dominant personalities, co-workers seek them out and listen to their opinions. They have an inborn gift for influencing others and using that gift in either positive or negative ways. With positive reinforcement, the gregarious second grader can become the high school class president. However, given negative reinforcement, the same dominant little leader organizes the bad boy pack.

People with an inherent aptitude for leadership tend to earn a position with a title. Those who find their way into a healthcare profession may become skilled providers and then progress to a leadership role. Others will find upper level leadership as directors of public relations, children's hospital department chiefs, or hospital foundation chairs. Recruiting, chairing committees and engaging other staff members comes easily for born leaders, and, whether or not they seek leadership, they remain leaders at heart. They consistently connect with co-workers and openly share suggestions for improving the work process.  Not only do they support the organization, but they also elevate the confidence and skills of co-workers.  By developing a comfortable two-way relationship with colleagues, they are able to set the stage for collaboration or sabotage within the group.  When an optimistic, favorable attitude is used, natural leaders will establish themselves as the go-to person and as a stabilizing anchor for the group.  Astute department chairs will quickly recognize the "opinion leaders" in the group and motivate them to use their inborn influence in an affirmative way.

Jasmin was born with an engaging personality.  In elementary school she sat in the front row and always had her hand up first.  On the playground, Jasmin had a group of loyal followers and always named the game that would be played.  In college, she earned a degree in nursing and was always the one in charge of student projects.  Not surprisingly, other students turned to her when they had questions about their studies.

After graduation, Jasmin joined a group of 54 nurses working in a busy hospital and consistent with her history, she quickly became a go-to person whose opinions were sought by her co-workers.  After a few years on the job, Jasmin was promoted to the nurse manager position.  Because she was respected by her peers as a de facto leader, she made the transition to leadership easily.  Once in place, Jasmin put an emphasis on maintaining a one on one connection with each member of the group.  She quickly engaged two other opinion leaders in the group to take on special projects.  By leveraging her connectedness and validating the talent of others on the team, Jasmin quickly gained the reputation of being an exceptional leader.

## Born Leaders ...

- Have a warm and welcoming personality
- Tend to draw others to them
- Are recognized as opinion leaders
- May have a positive or negative attitude

## ...With a Positive attitude

- Openly support colleagues and encourage personal growth
- Seek collective excellence
- Visualize and implement changes to benefit clients and co-workers
- Celebrate success of the team

## ...with a negative attitude

- Sabotage the team's success
- Harm the larger organization
- Undermine your leadership

## Drawbacks

Being a born leader has potential drawbacks.  Natural leaders tend to be put on a pedestal by their co-workers and often are assumed to know more than they actually know.  In an effort to preserve an image of being the perfect leader, they are tempted to give answers and opinions that sound logical but may not be based in fact.  Additionally, an opinion leader who is elevated to a leadership position may have difficulty taking on the actual leadership role.  Because the natural leader has always been the frontline achiever, she may have difficulty giving tasks to others or sharing credit for success.

If you were born with a magnetic personality and you find yourself on the pathway to leadership, use your gifts wisely.   Natural leaders are seldom shy or timid.  Use your outgoing personality to develop poise and confidence in administrative settings and negotiations.  Make a commitment to build on your innate talents realizing that you will be judged by the success of your team, because without your team, it's not possible to be successful.  Develop a sincere desire to elevate each member of the team and adhere strictly to integrity, honesty and transparency.  By combining your history of being an opinion leader with a commitment to learning and applying leadership skills, your career will emerge in a powerful way.

## Planned Leader

A Planned Leader is one who establishes leadership as a career goal and actively seeks opportunities to lead.  You may be born to lead, or determined to lead or you may have been placed on a leadership pathway by your organization who wants you to lead. Nevertheless, rather than relying on natural ability, planned leaders actively seek and embrace opportunities to learn leadership skills. In his book, *Leading The Life You Want*, Stewart Friedman downplays the born leader philosophy, emphasizing that a lot of hard work goes into becoming a leader. He notes that through hard work and commitment, people who want to be leaders can learn the skills needed to be successful. Even so, a Planned Leader plans a career route, establishes the viable path to leadership and does the work to achieve the goal.

Some of you on the planned route may already be in a leadership position and are actively expanding your skills to enhance your leadership abilities. Others of you may have recently earned a leadership position and are now learning new skills needed for success. Regardless of your current position or how long you have been there, your leadership is ever evolving and expanding. An organized study of leadership skills will augment your planned pathway and increase your chances for further growth. Begin with a focus in two areas, building self-confidence and refining your current expertise.

**Display confidence.** While continuing your academic study of leadership, make it a priority to learn how to convey a physical image of self-confidence. It is generally believed that we only get one chance to make a first impression and the experts in psychology and in business literature agree with the importance of making a positive first impression. To develop self-confidence in preparation for all interactions with the chain of command, do the following.

- Maintain a healthy, pleasant appearance.

- Practice the body language associated with leadership.
- Be a regular speaker inside or outside the industry.
- Volunteer to be the head of a charity event.
- Be physically active in a recreational sport.

Writing in the forbes.com blog, author, Carol Kinsey Goman notes that if your body looks closed, depressed or angry, the postures will be subconsciously picked up and mimicked by your team. She refers to the process as "emotional contagion." The emotional contagion of your leadership will set the emotional tone for the group and can work either in a positive or negative way. When you act decisively and speak with confidence, when you carry yourself well and gesture with intent, upper level management senses that you have everything under control and that you will emerge with the same poise in leadership.

**Refine your expertise.**   Planned leaders have a vision of becoming a leader. Rather than making a commitment to simply securing a leadership position, make a commitment to developing your leadership skills so you are ready to follow through on your planned pathway. Taking a position just to obtain a leadership title may put you in the wrong job. Avoid being a title-seeker by doing a self-assessment to review your motivation and long term goals, then ask yourself, "Where does the current position fit into that goal?" With self-reflection, your leadership role will have a purpose moving you toward your greater vision. Once you know the purpose of your position, make an all-in commitment to do the following.

- Serving and supporting your team
- Empowering each team member

- Supporting the mission, vision and values of the larger organization
- Continuing to learn about leadership skills
- Seeking a mentor

**The plan to become a leader requires active learning.** Study leadership with confidence, commitment and organization as you build a solid foundation of leadership skills. Examine your motives and ask yourself tough questions about why you want a leadership position. Are you a self-serving leader with the ulterior motive of trying to promote yourself, or are you a serving leader who genuinely wants to elevate a team of workers? If you cannot commit to serving your team and the greater organization, then your plan for leadership is all about you, not the team. As you will continue to learn throughout this book, *your* success is tied to *team* success. Dedicate yourself to the team to ensure your personal success.

## Selected Leaders

A selected leader is one who has been *selected* through an application process to fill a specific need. A selected leader should anticipate going through an established selection process. Depending upon the type of organization and the requirements of the position, the interview and selection could be done by a small committee or voted on by every member of the organization, or by some process between. In healthcare, the selection is often made by a department chair in consultation with a team of upper level managers. The department frequently prefers to hire from within, but for key positions, a selection committee may be formed and the position will be advertised both regionally and nationally. When the institution does a regional or national search, the desired outcome is to have a pool of highly qualified applicants for the committee to interview before making a final selection.

The most competitive applicants are those who have developed a plan (Planned Leader) that includes improving management skills and gaining credentials to support the selection for leadership. The person with a focus on selected leadership will probably have earned a PhD or an MBA with the intent of being promoted to leadership. The employer will want to see that your work experience that includes a progression of responsibility. In addition to advanced degrees and significant experience, your depth of knowledge in management, communication and negotiating topics makes you a stronger candidate. Selected Leadership is not a quick or easy process. An extension of planned leadership, it requires an ongoing commitment to acquiring knowledge, skills and experience as well as respectful patience with the process.

**Selected Leaders...**

- Actively pursue selection for leadership
- Are knowledgeable about the organization, its mission and vision
- Have studied the fields of leadership and teambuilding
- Welcome the title and value leadership
- Sincerely want to make a positive difference
- Are eager to use their leadership skills

- Are patient through the process

## Diverging Pathways

*Emerging Leaders* and *Appointed Leaders* fit among the other more specific paths of Born, Planned and Selected leadership. An emerging leader is one who is in the beginning phases of any first-time, and perhaps permanent, leadership role. Bringing in a leader from the outside can be costly in terms of time and money therefore new leaders commonly emerge to be selected from within the existing workgroup. If a person with seniority has enough preparation for the role and has a sincere desire to serve the group, the organization will benefit from having a person who knows the system.

Rather than promoting an "emerging leader" based on seniority, a more common scenario is to identify and promote a solid worker who is recognized as a born leader but not necessarily a planned one. The assumption is that competence in patient care will translate into competence as a leader, an assumption that may or may not be true. Out of loyalty to both the institution and co-workers, the person may "emerge" to reluctantly accept the position without embracing the leadership role. Rather than taking charge, the reluctant leader is likely to assure the group that everything is still the same. But if an initially reticent worker who has accepted an emerging leadership position embraces the job and commits to learning new skills, good things can happen.

If you are a newly emerging leader who accepted a position out of loyalty to the group, you may be saying, "Whoa, what have I done!"

It's time to take a deep breath and realize that if you have a history of accepting challenges and mastering the skills for success, you are not in this position by chance. The variety of skills and your potential for leadership have been observed and management thinks you can do it. When you commit, you're saying, "Yes, I will do it."

**You were selected because**

- Your loyalty to the organization is known.
- Your work to date is recognized and appreciated.
- Your supervisor believes that you can grow into the leadership role.
- You have a working knowledge of the workflow.
- Your work supports the mission and vision of the organization.

Depending upon the urgency of filling the position and the resources of the organization, a different type of selection occurs when a group of mid to upper-level leaders meet, review their talent pool, and appoint the person they feel will best lead the team. Appointed leaders meet some vital needs of the larger organization. Your new leadership position confirms that your abilities are recognized and that you are trusted to follow organizational goals while motivating your team. Those who appointed you to your leadership position have a vested interest in your success. They need you to be successful. By accepting the appointment, you are in a unique position to fulfill an organizational need as well as satisfying the needs of your team.

**Leverage your position to assure your success as an appointed leader in the following ways.**

- Seek a mentor.
- Arrange for functional office space.
- Plan for adequate administrative time.
- Negotiate with the organization take a leadership course.
- Schedule concrete time for team-building.
- Build a mechanism to showcase your team.

Regardless of whether you eagerly or reluctantly emerged in a leadership role, it is within your control to leverage the position and achieve worthy results. Success does not depend upon the skills that you bring into your new job but rather on your ability and willingness to learn. Exude confidence as you apply the leadership skills taught in this book and your team will be more effective than you ever thought possible.

## Interim Leaders

*"Interim leadership is a delicate blend of opportunity and risk."*

An Interim Leader is one who is asked to serve for a stipulated period between the departure of one leader and prior to the selection of another.  There are many reasons why a current position becomes available and an interim is appointed, and an equal number of potential outcomes.  On the plus side, the experience can serve as an interview for permanent promotion or it can be a way to "give back" to the organization.  As well, interim positions have negative consequences.  A popular leader who leaves because of illness or injury may leave a sad and stressed team behind for the interim leader to help through their grief.  If a departing popular leader retires or leaves for another position inside or outside the organization, the leadership shoes may be difficult to fill, even on the interim basis. In other situations an ineffective leader may have been asked to step down and the interim leader inherits a team that has lost confidence in leadership, placing the interim in a tenuous position.  However, many leaders simply get promoted and move on, leaving an opportunity for another leader to emerge and turn a good situation into an even better one.

Serving as an interim leader requires a special type of person who can connect with the group quickly while supporting institutional goals and initiatives.  It could be a born leader with a gift in leadership or a planned leader who is prepared for, and perhaps experienced in, leadership.  When the length of the interim position is known, it is easy to set an agenda and for your boss to give you a list of expectations that go with the temporary position.   If a search is under way and applications are being taken, the duration of the interim position may be offered as open-ended.  Regardless of the time span, the interim leader should have a personality and style that quickly engages team members and motivates them.  As discussed throughout this book, a successful leader must have a vision. For the interim leader who is given a limited amount of time in the leadership role, a logical short term vision is to set the stage for the permanent leader who will follow. By sharing the vision with the team and encouraging their participation, the new leader will create a team that eagerly anticipates the arrival of the new leader.

There are three primary kinds of interim leader - *caretaker, fully engaged* and *transition.* The kind the employer needs is based on the authority you are to be given and the expectations that will be placed upon you, and will be determined by the circumstances surrounding your selection. In some cases the interim leader is only expected to maintain the status quo until a full time person is named. When the interim position covers a longer span of time, the leader is expected to move the group forward. In other situations, the interim leader is brought in from the outside to implement an unpopular change that will set the permanent leader up for success. Each interim position requires a unique set of leadership skills and though it offers few guarantees for the future, it may open many opportunities.


**The caretaker interim leader** is most commonly appointed to fill a gap when the current leader makes a short notice exit and the new person has not yet arrived. Frequently, the caretaker interim leader is a person who was selected and appointed or promoted from within. This person is already on the team, role models behavior that is favorable to upper administration, and can be trusted to maintain the status quo until a permanent leader is put into place. More often than not when a caretaker leader is appointed, there is a formal search currently under way for a permanent leader. If you are asked to be a caretaker interim leader while a search is being conducted, you may be eligible, or be advised, to apply for the full time position. Regardless, for the interim leader, goals are set by the institution and success is measured by the day to day workflow continuing without interruption.

An example of a caretaker interim leader is one of my former assistant chiefs. He was an exceptional frontline healthcare provider whose team was in need of leadership while a national search for the right candidate was underway. Administrative support was in place to help carry out the day to day management, but, the team needed a designated leader. Already in a part-time leadership role, the assistant accepted the position on an interim basis to ensure that the group kept its identity. He also made sure that forms were signed and schedules were posted. In this position, the interim leader was not expected to create or implement policy, but rather to support policy, and to maintain order within the group until the national search was complete.

**The fully engaged interim leader** is most often a high achiever from within the group who is respected by both upper level management and peers. Although an interim leader, this person is expected to fully embrace the position as if it were permanent. Connecting with team members, developing policies and moving the organizational mission forward are all expectations. A fully engaged interim is expected to move beyond maintaining status quo to providing active leadership. The fully engaged interim leader takes charge and functions as a short-term permanent leader.

**Success Story**. As a born leader who was well-respected by her peers, Kelley was the natural selection as an interim leader when the long term permanent leader retired. Although the former leader had done a commendable job, the period leading up to retirement found her treading water in the job and having lost the desire to develop new initiatives that she would not be there long enough to complete. For 6 months the group was stagnant. Kelley willingly accepted the interim position and immediately took responsibility for the daily administrative tasks. Because of her experience as a frontline worker, she knew first-hand a few things that could be changed to improve the workflow. She engaged her group to participate in several projects and delegated responsibility to team members. As a result of engaged leadership, both the productivity and morale of the group improved. Kelley applied for the permanent position, and in recognition of her leadership skills, she was awarded the leadership job. Following the appointment, upper level leadership revealed that Kelley had been their choice for the permanent position all along, but because she was relatively young, they had placed her in a trial situation where she could prove herself before being appointing her to leadership.

**The transition interim leader** is a person who is brought in from outside the workgroup for a specific purpose. In some cases, the interim leader is tasked with implementing changes that will position a permanent leader for success. These changes may be popular, or more likely, unpopular. When upper level management makes the pragmatic decision to hire a transition leader to implement unpopular change, the interim's leadership is accompanied by high risk and low reward.

The transition person who is placed in an interim position specifically to make unpopular changes can expect to receive passive/aggressive push back from the team and to quickly become a target for sabotage. He may be viewed as a professional gunslinger, hired to cause harm. In the following story, one of my previous employers got mixed results while using an interim leader to implement a revised benefits package.

With changes in reimbursement due to healthcare regulations, the employer was forced to change the benefits package in order for the organization to remain solvent.  What was once an exceptional benefits package needed to be cut back.  An effort was made to be competitive with others in the area, but it was still a definite step down from the existing benefits.  In the process of designing a new benefits package to meet the criteria of the Board of Directors, the administrative director stepped down and an interim was put in place specifically to roll out the reduced benefits package.  The new package was revealed and, as expected, the interim had alienated established staff and become the most distrusted person in the organization. Two years later a permanent administrative director was selected who inherited the new benefits package already in place.  Having started with a clean slate, the new administrator received none of the blame for the reduction in benefits and none of the animosity.  In this case, an interim leader served a specific purpose, implemented the new policy with a heavy hand, and was asked to move on.

Whether or not to accept any interim position depends entirely upon the situation that you inherit.  In Kelley's case, it was a great experience that led to a permanent position with a highly engaged workgroup.  In the case of the administrative director, the interim leader willingly became distrusted and the least liked person in the organization and, though he was happy to go, everyone was happy he left.  The caretaker who fills in as a manager for a specific timeframe may have a modestly pleasant experience and the short term transition interim who fills an interim position while acting as a consultant may enjoy every minute.  The key to a successful interim experience is for the employer and employee to mutually understand the rules and to put it all in writing.

**Clarify the expectations of your interim role.** Use these tips to clarify the goals and expectations that the institution has of you while in the temporary position. Before accepting an interim position, you must address these issues.

- Establish the duration of position.
- Define whether you will be a caretaker, fully engaged or transitional interim leader.
- Agree on any policy changes that you are expected to make as an interim.
- Determine whether or not you are eligible to apply for the full time position.
- Negotiate a compensation package appropriate for your new responsibility.
- Get it in writing.

## The Nutshell

Selecting a new leader is an important and yet commonly overlooked opportunity to build a team that supports the greater mission and vision of the organization. The strength of the entire organization depends on placing talented leaders like you in the right place at the right time. But where will they find you? Which pathway are you on?

**Are you a natural?**

Born Leaders have dynamic and sometimes larger than life personalities that influence those around them. They were born to be at the head of the class, leading it one direction or the other. By pacing themselves and holding their egos in check, born leaders who choose to use their natural gifts while learning about leadership, can be highly effective leading teams of healthcare workers.

**Are you a seeker?**

Planned Leaders have a deep-seated desire to become a leader and they commit early on to developing the necessary skills and the contacts in order to become effective. Formal education programs, independent studies, and teaming with a trusted mentor are useful tools in opening the doors to successful career leadership.

**Are you in active pursuit?**

Selected Leaders actively seek leadership positions through application, interview and selection. The inside or outside applicant who is selected for leadership will have advanced credentials and up to date knowledge of the mission, vision and nuances of the organization.

**Are you a stop-gap risk taker?**

Interim Leaders are appointed as placeholders between two leaders and may or may not be offered the full-time position. They may be signing up for a challenging ride through the unknown or for a well-defined short-term opportunity to lead. If you are offered an interim position, protect yourself by asking questions and agreeing ahead of time on duration, expectations and compensation.

By reading *Leader Reader 1* you are already on a pathway, emerging as a leader. Tap your talents and make yourself known; continue on your pathway and be ready to step up to the plate. Where can "those tasked with hiring find effective leaders?" They look for people on a Pathway to Leadership. They look for leaders like you.

# Chapter 4

# Leadership Skills

What is the single most important skill that will help guarantee your success as a leader? Answer that question and you have found the holy grail of leadership. Professional golfers are allowed to have 14 clubs in their bag. On tournament day, each golfer must assess the course, consider the weather conditions and then load the bag with the clubs that are expected to be the most useful under the circumstances. Each time a golfer takes the course, the bag is loaded differently depending on the lay of the land.

Like mastering a variety of golf shots, a bag of skills are required for effective leadership, and the challenge of the day will determine which skills will be most useful. Being confident and proficient in a variety of techniques opens the door to success. This chapter introduces multiple handy skills for the new leader, and the savvy one, as you pick up your game bag and head out to conquer the course.

## Organize Your Time and Space

*"Never confuse activity with results."*

Being a frontline healthcare leader means you work in a very chaotic and demanding environment where every minute counts. Organizing your space and your time is essential for your survival. You will work more efficiently, and, you will create the accurate appearance of having things under control.

I have a confession to make.  Organizing space and time did not come naturally to me.  Having good intent and working massive hours were a great rationalization in those early days, but as I advanced to leadership, I had to resolve the problem. You will find, as I did, that as your responsibility grows and your life becomes more complex, being disorganized is like pushing a snowball uphill. As disorganization increases, the snowball gains mass and becomes harder and harder to push.  You don't want to wait for it to roll backward and crush you in the process.

Fortunately for me, my wife has a talent for organization and is a helpful mentor.  On one occasion, we pulled out my overfilled desk drawer, laid a blanket on the home office floor, emptied the contents onto the blanket and arranged everything in identifiable groups.  For five minutes each evening I sorted and filed, throwing significantly more than I kept, and easily finished by the end of the week.  By setting up a time schedule for eliminating the dust catchers from tops of desks and shelves and losing the fear of throwing things away, my productivity vastly improved.  When you try to take care of business in a cluttered space, you can work for hours with very little to show for the time spent.  By working in a clean space while following a schedule with specific goals for each time block, I can now accomplish twice as much in half the time. When done with a task, I cross it off the day's work list; then I delete the list! If you are like I was as a young leader and have difficulty with organization, get help if you need it, but clean the clutter and commit to working in a neat and organized space. Here are some tips.

- **De-clutter your workspace.** Set aside a block of time to clean your work space. Because experienced leaders tend to accumulate documents and other muddle as space permits, new leaders frequently inherit a workspace that includes file cabinets filled to capacity. Whether you are experienced or new, block an hour – or two - of your time for office cleaning. Start with your desk and remove everything from the desktop. Empty the drawers. Wipe the spaces clean and put back ONLY the things that you truly need. Just because you inherited it doesn't mean you need it. Be ruthless and "when in doubt, throw it out."
- **Cleanse the cabinets.** In a recent new leadership position, I took possession of file cabinets that had information dating back 10-15 years. I quickly realized that notes from a safety meeting 8 years ago were of no value. Purging the office began with a resolution that "...anything over 2 years old is no longer relevant and must be tossed." As the recycle bin filled, my file space emptied and in the next two years, nothing that was removed was missed. A functioning office is not meant to be a museum or a storeroom. Your work space is your home base.
- **Sack the paper.** It is frustrating to be home and need information that is in a file cabinet in your office, but fortunately, we live in a digital age where you may have instant access to information through your computer. First, you need to know the rules and regulations of your institution regarding the storage and transport of information. Many institutions require that all job related information be stored on their server and, if so, make sure

that you have remote access and can view information from home.  Other organizations allow you to store information on a personal flash drive as long as the material does not include patient data or violate HIPPA regulations.  My own preference is to put important files related to managing the team on a personal flash drive.  Having easy access to policies and procedures regardless of your location enables you to have 24/7 oversight of your workgroup.  Over the past 10 years the vast majority of non-secure work related information travels with me on my personal flash drive which I back up weekly to a storage device.

## "Being organized may literally save your leadership career."

- **Make a daily schedule.**  When you arrive at work in the morning, you have many tasks on your to-do list and you may be relaxed knowing that you have a full day to complete the tasks.  Then at the end of a hectic day, you may look at your list and realize that several important things were not accomplished.  Being busy is not always being productive.  As a healthcare leader, especially on the frontline, you will always have plenty of distractions to take your attention from important issues.  An empowering lesson that I learned early in my leadership career is to take the time to make and follow a schedule.   There's more detail later in the chapter covering the end of day routine but, for now, recognize that your shut-down procedure should include organizing for tomorrow.  Ending each day by making a list of things to accomplish tomorrow will increase the odds for having another productive day. When I arrive in the morning, I review my list from the day before and add anything that popped up overnight, after which I make out an hour by hour schedule for the day based on priorities. If you follow this procedure and cross off completed items one by one, at the end of the day it will be easy to document the use of your time. Making and adhering to a schedule is efficient and simple in an ideal workplace, however, we live in the real world where the unanticipated occurs suddenly. After having my best-laid plans regularly ambushed with spur of the moment problems, I learned to add two blocks of time for the Crisis of the Day (COD). I block 30 minutes in the morning and a full hour in the afternoon to deal with the unexpected, but predictable, COD. By reserving time on the schedule for issues that emerge unexpectedly, I am able to keep on schedule with the other important items.

- **Make a list of 3-minute tasks.** Three minutes may seem like such a short time, however, there are many important things that can be done quickly. The small break you have between meetings or agenda items can be used to accomplish these simple tasks. Keeping a second list of short tasks will remind to make use of every minute. What can you do in 3-5 minutes? Clean today's clutter from your desk, transfer files to a flash drive, transfer notes from paper to a digital file, update your calendar, start your list of items for tomorrow, reply to an email. You are the expert when it comes to the demands of your job. Create your own list of 3-minute jobs and use it to fill the small gaps in your schedule.
- **Create a pending folder.** Rather than having scraps of paper on your desk, have one folder where you put all of your

notes regarding items in need of your review. Better yet, create a digital file on your flash drive. If you don't want to use a flash drive, apps are available for your phone or pad that will help you organize tasks. By organizing pending items into a folder or digital file, you are able to keep your space clean.

## Make a Small Difference Immediately

### *"Establish yourself as a leader by quickly making small changes to the status quo."*

One of the biggest mistakes that a new leader can make, especially one who was promoted from within the workgroup, is to try to convince the group that you are the same old person and "nothing has changed." Nothing could be further from the truth. For one thing, you have a new title and the team is counting on you to step up and be the leader. And the boss did not select you for leadership with hopes that nothing would change. Assure your team of your "thereness" by being assertive in a positive way and make a few small but visible changes soon after taking the position. You may be unsure where to start but your team knows exactly what to change immediately to produce a positive effect on both morale and workflow. Allow them to tell you. As soon as possible after taking charge of your group, schedule a town hall meeting where you can openly discuss issues. Ask your team what is most important to them both short and long term. Identify things that can be changed now as well as things that will need to change over time. Listen attentively to the group and walk away with one or two changes that you will implement quickly. Now you know where to start, and when your team feels certain that they were heard, and that voicing their ideas made a difference, they will line up to support you. By listening and then acting, you're letting the team know that they matter and you will instill a sense of optimism regarding the outcome of collaborative work. Consider the following.

- Whether or not you are new at leadership, if you were promoted from within the clinical arena, you have been a peer for a period of time. As a co-worker, you were likely recognized for your excellence delivering patient care and you need to keep your skills honed. Maintain a clinical presence to demonstrate that your new role has not affected your clinical competence. With a management position, your clinical time may be restricted, but maintaining your skills in the clinical arena will make a difference to your team.
- Be empathetic and stay connected one on one to send the immediate message to the team that each person is important and respected. If you were promoted from within a group, you have the advantage of already knowing the people on the team and can build on existing relationships. If you were brought in from the outside, you face the challenge of very quickly establishing personal relationships with each individual in the group. Does this mean that you need to be their best buddy? Absolutely not. It is to your advantage to know each member of the group on a personal level and get to know what motivates them, but being a best friend does not have to be a goal. Most of your workgroup

do not want you as a best friend either, but they do expect you to know and understand their needs.
- People are motivated and feel valued when you build upon their creative ideas.  At the town hall meeting you can validate the individual and motivate the group by posing a question such as, "What would it take to gain the reputation of being the best workgroup in the organization?" Encourage everybody to participate and listen to all input. As the meeting progresses and enthusiasm increases, ask the group to identify several things that could be done immediately to move the group toward the goal; then listen attentively again.  Let the group agree on 1-2 focus items and over the next few weeks work with the group to achieve resolution.  You gain credibility as a new leader and develop accountability among your team when you act quickly on the issues that are most important to the team.  At a subsequent town hall meeting, review the progress and have the team identify an additional focus area.  Build success upon success.

## Create and Share your Vision

*"An inspiring vision gives direction, enhances teamwork and empowers creativity."*

Who is the greatest leader in history?   Most people will have trouble naming a single person, except maybe Muhammad Ali, as "...the greatest."  It's probably easier to make a list of several people whom you consider to be exceptional leaders.  As you create the list, look for this common characteristic to emerge: The ability to create and share a vision.  Unlike managers who are charged with efficiently organizing the staff jobs for the day, leaders must inspire and motivate people to follow a common vision and achieve specific goals.  Let's look at the importance of having a vision.

John F. Kennedy was elected as the 35th President of the United States in 1960 and quickly captured the support of the American public because he was young, dynamic and well-respected as a hero of World War II.  Throughout his campaign for office and early into the Presidency, Kennedy had a vision of American greatness and he openly invited the public to participate.   One component of his vision involved the health of the population, so Kennedy introduced the President's physical fitness award for participation in a standard fitness exercise program.  In short order, school children all across America were starting the day with the "Chicken Fat Song."   JFK also had a long range vision that engaged and captivated the nation.  In a speech on September 12, 1962, Kennedy stated, "By the end of the decade we will send a man to the moon and safely return him to earth."  The entire USA embraced this vision and the space race was launched.

Less famous people have had a vision and engaged public support, permanently changing the way we live our lives.  At a time when New York City was isolated on the island of Manhattan, the famous bridge-builder, John Roebling, had a vision for building a structure to span the East River, connecting Manhattan with the borough of Brooklyn.  After putting the project on paper, the elder Roebling passed away and his son, Washington, became the chief engineer for implementing his father's vision. The bridge would be a massive structure and able to withstand the elements of wind and floods. In a time of rampant political corruption, Washington Roebling faced the challenge of avoiding New York politics while bringing communities on both shores together to support and believe in the project. Roebling's singular focus became a relentless effort toward achieving the final outcome. In 1883, the Roebling vision for a great Brooklyn Bridge became a reality and still stands today.

Those are great stories about men with a vision, however, as a healthcare leader you probably aren't going to the moon quite yet, but you are using the leadership skills that build bridges. You are building on your vision for a cohesive team that transports the highest quality of care possible to your patients. In order for your team to function at its full potential, they must develop and embrace a common vision. A meaningful vision for your team must address what your team is tasked to accomplish. Assess where you and your team are right now (status quo) and where you would like to be in the future (your vision). Openly share your thoughts and welcome the group's feedback as the vision is clarified. When your vision has become everyone's vision, be sure you role-model the behavior that will move your team toward that end. Here is how vision worked for one large healthcare team.

**Story Lesson** A major healthcare organization, known for offering superior quality of care, had difficulty recruiting staff due to its location in a small town. The specialty team of 46 members within the organization was highly regarded for their competence and skills, but still had difficulty attracting applicants. They could not change their hospital location so they changed their work environment. To elevate morale, a new leader, who was committed to providing direction, was assigned to the team to improve recruiting techniques. The new leader proposed a vision and engaged the group to share in it with the agreement that all future decisions would be based on achieving that goal. The vision was simple: To be the healthcare employer of choice in the State. This simple vision stimulated discussion among the group about what it would look like if, in fact, they were the employer of choice. The group became more cohesive and eagerly discussed topics related to the work environment and the interaction within their team. After forthright discussion, the group decided they would *actively* create a place where people enjoyed coming to work each day. Working together, they identified *interaction* and *trust in each other* as the key elements in achieving that specific goal, and each team member pledged to be a model for the required elements. A special emphasis was placed on engaging and teaching the desired behavior to each new hire added to the group. Soon after, people began holding one another accountable for their actions, and, as they did so, a sense of community with a common purpose emerged. A shared and common vision made the difference, and within a year there were more applicants than openings on the team.

Be an effective leader and motivate your team by introducing a vision and challenging them to fine-tune it as necessary, then to support it until it becomes the mantra, accepted by all. Your shared team vision is the instrument that provides direction for your decisions. When developing a vision, take the following concepts into consideration.

- **Know the values of the larger organization.** Your team's vision must embrace, align with, and support the mission, vision and core values of the larger organization. If the organization has short term initiatives under way, incorporate them into your group vision.

- **Know the special needs and challenges of your team.** Listen carefully to your team members as they express both creative ideas and concerns. A vision that addresses issues that are important to the team is much more likely to generate support and engagement.
- **Keep your vision fresh by reviewing it annually with your team.** What has been achieved? What new challenges have emerged? If the current vision is still valid, what can be done to take it to the next level? Posing questions to your team and then actively listening will provide you with insight and, at the same time, will validate and motivate your team members.

## Empower, Engage, and Energize your Team

*"By engaging and inspiring, a great boss will make the team feel smarter and more valuable."*

Healthcare leaders are actively busy people tasked with the day to day operation of a workgroup while, at the same time, ensuring that a patient population receives quality care from a committed team. High expectations are placed on the leader simultaneously by the team and the organization. Therefore, leaders at all levels ask, "What is the most important thing I can do to inspire my team?" The most important thing you can do is be physically present and connect with every member of the team. Rather than using a single skill, build your leadership foundation on the 3 E's

***Empower, Engage, and Energize*** in order to put yourself on the right track to satisfy the patients, the organization and your team.

Psychologists who study the workplace environment have done surveys to provide information about what makes an organization a great place for a person to work. Surprisingly, top pay is rarely on the list of most important factors from the employee's perspective. Although fair pay is important, being empowered to work using full capability is the need that commonly tops the list, along with a sense of being valued by both the organization and by a supervisor. With those conclusions in mind, learn from the research and resolve to help empower each individual on your team to work at their highest potential. The payoff comes when creative talent is unleashed, substantially increasing morale and productivity.

## Build on the 3 E's

Empowerment transpires when your team members feel that they are free to carry out job-related tasks knowing that you trust and encourage their decisions. When you handle it correctly, empowerment suffuses your team with a sense of ownership and pride in a job well done. Here are some tips for developing empowerment.

- **Believe in your team.** Team members have received formal education in the profession and they are licensed and eager to do a good job. Avoid being a micromanager and release the power of your team by providing resources and guidance, then stay out of the way and give them the space to do the job. Set clear goals and expectations about the required outcome, but be ready to step back and allow the group to identify and solve problems. Having confidence in the competence of your team will motivate and elevate them to a high level of performance. In the words of General George Patton, "Never tell people how to do things. Tell them what needs to be done and they will surprise you with their ingenuity."

- **Encourage and promote professional growth.** In addition to their famous political polls, Gallup is known for surveys of corporate workforces that assess the level of engagement of employees within an organization. Two decades ago, Gallup administered a lengthy survey to each employee of several hundred companies to assess employee engagement. The survey was designed to assess whether or not an employer recognizes and values the contributions of the individual worker. Over the years, the survey was refined and Gallup was able to shorten the survey to 12 statements with which the respondent must agree or disagree on a scale of 1 to 10. One of the 12 survey statements reads, "Someone at work encourages my development." As the survey improved, Gallup learned that an essential element of effective leadership is *showing belief in each individual member of the team.*

A tangible way to show that you appreciate each individual team member is to develop a plan for each person to grow professionally. Making a growth plan involves a one-on-one discussion to assure that the plan is tailored to the person's needs. An effective plan starts with the individual's self-assessment and is followed by exploring where the person wants to grow professionally. A proactive and organized way to develop a growth plan is to make it part of the person's annual review; schedule a 6-month follow up to keep the plan focused on the result. It is both supportive and reassuring when you adjust a team member's work hours to accommodate taking a class or attending a seminar. Believing in and supporting the growth of each individual will pay big dividends in the long run.

- **Be a mentor and a coach.** No doubt, you are successful because someone took enough interest in your career to help you develop confidence and skills. Leaders are in a unique position to do the same for the members of a team. Team members with different levels of experience need different types of mentoring. Some staff will be entry level professionals who will need a coach throughout the orientation process. Others will be more experienced, having mastered the basic skills necessary for success as healthcare providers. Your more experienced team members are the future leaders for your organization and will benefit from having a mentoring relationship with you. "Engage and empower" by taking an interest in their professional development and include leadership and management mentoring for those who display a gift for leadership. Not only will your team be energized, you will have people within the group to help you share some of the administrative burden.

- **Recognize and reward success.** From early childhood we are taught about fairness as we learn to put forth extra effort with the expectation that greater contribution means greater rewards. Your team members also expect recognition and reward for jobs well done, large and small. Should we have a "trophy kid" mentality in the workplace? Emphatically, no! Rewards need to be earned, but it is essential to celebrate success for all levels of achievement. Ordinary every day activities can be rewarded with a sincere thank you, and greater recognition can be reserved for larger achievements.  Having a Kudos Board in the department lounge provides an opportunity to note excellence in a spontaneous and ongoing manner.  You can start team meetings by pointing out successes of team members.  When the team works together for a major event such as accreditation, a group reward has been earned.  Celebrate success with a crawfish boil, a bowling night, or an event at a local park, anything that brings the team together and encourages them to enthusiastically take on the next challenge.  Hosting an annual team retreat is another opportunity to review successes, to recognize individuals and set the agenda for the upcoming year.  Be proactive about securing the necessary funding for ongoing rewards and an annual retreat.

Leadership is a contact sport that requires each team member to perceive a personal connection with you as their leader.  Actively engage the team to co-create the agenda for positive change and then believe in each person.  Releasing their creative energy will produce amazing results.  If you want to empower, engage and energize your team, first listen to them and then provide the resources and encouragement necessary to complete each task.

## Lead by Example

***"The way you conduct your business is the lesson that you teach to your team"***

A constant motif in *Leader Reader 1* is:  Lead from an internal foundation of integrity.  Leadership is very visible and your integrity is on constant display.  When you lead with integrity, when you align your deeds with your words, you earn credibility.  The Emerson quote, "What you do screams so loudly that I can't hear what you say," is just as true now as when it was first written.  In addition to controlling your own actions and listening to your own words, your team is watching and listening to you, too.  They perceive your tone, the depth of your sincerity, and the self-confidence you have because of doing what you believe.  Your allegiance to the team is demonstrated by the sum total of your behavior.

- **Be consistent and reliable.**  Everything you do and say must align with your core values.  Be on time and come prepared for work and for meetings.  Keep the team schedule up to date and make sure the vacation schedule is accurate and available to view.  Have a modified open door policy – red light, green light - that is understood and respected by everyone.  Follow all organization policy from safety concerns to length of work day.  If you're a frontline leader, implement all patient safety protocol and keep your credentials up to date.  Core values must be identifiable in everything that you say and do.  A leader who displays a double standard is doomed to failure, or worse.
- **Display self-confidence**  How you enter a room, how you greet a stranger or a co-worker, how you dress, how you manage hand gestures and "carry" your body all send a loud message to those around you.  There is wide consensus among psychologists supporting the concept that tone and

body language are more important than the content. You can generate confidence by practicing and displaying the language of leadership.

- **Set the emotional tone.** It isn't just what you say but how you say it. Our brains are set up to process both emotional and intellectual data and your team wants a leader who is in control of both. Regardless of what you say to your team, if you appear stressed or off balance, your team will lose confidence in your ability to lead. Losing your temper, using or tolerating foul language, overreacting to stress and obligation are all signs that you lack emotional fortitude. The strength you show during leadership's high pressure pace cools the air and establishes calm. Here are some strong and reassuring behaviors you can use. In order to set the tone:
    - Walk in the door with high energy each day.
    - Use setbacks as opportunities.
    - Diffuse sticky situations by keeping fingers off the hot buttons, theirs and yours.
    - Announce birthdays and birth news joyfully.
    - Admonish team members privately and constructively.
    - Deliver sad news and bad news without doom and gloom, maintaining the continuity of the team after a tragedy.
    - Never fire someone publicaly and keep the details to yourself.

Your team looks to you for the example of desired behavior. Have an open and receptive attitude and make your work place a place where respectful candor is protected.   The following are behaviors that are critical for you to teach by your example and for your team to imitate.

## Influence Others

### "If you don't use your own power to influence, someone else will."

Influence is powerful. Healthcare professionals are influenced by a set of megastars – the CEOs, the directors, the board members, the foundation members and philanthropists, the department directors and by leaders like YOU.  With your influence, you are able to personally affect the actions of others, in fact, some would argue there is no leadership without it.  A leader who is not able to sway the opinion of others or change their behavior, is really just a manager who is keeping the papers in order.   If you do not develop your ability to influence your team, they will lack direction and never rise to their potential.

New leaders often make the mistake of thinking that influence is something that can only be earned and developed over time and that they are powerless when first hired.  It is true that your impact on people will grow as you become established in your position, however, by having received a leadership position, you already have credibility. Those above you in the chain of command expect your input, thereby, inviting you to exert your influence.   Each time you use your position as a tool to enhance the entire group, your impact increases. Here are some tips for growing your influence.

- **Use facts to persuade.** "Because I said so," is never the right answer to give when you're trying to persuade others. Instead, prepare and present the facts. Your team members are smart and deserve to know the background behind the decision and you don't need to fear their resistance. Use facts to clarify a misunderstanding and to support any new initiative under way. When sharing facts, never assume that you have them all and be open to the possibility that someone may have new information to share with you. Using facts to persuade is most effective when it is a two-way collaborative process in which each individual has the opportunity to learn and grow. Because being forthright involves more than giving information to your team, ensure that all stakeholders are informed, especially your supervisor. If you have specific information about a pending decision, sharing your facts with the chain of command increases the likelihood for a better decision. Neither your team nor your boss likes to be surprised.
- **Seek advice.** Something very interesting happens when you ask another person for their advice. Not only are you able to view the situation from a different perspective but often the person takes an interest in the challenge you face. In a collaborative environment, the person not only gives advice but may offer to help you resolve the issue as well. New leaders often make the mistake of being too selective in using the perfect person to consult. Avoid being locked into the notion that the best advice always comes from the front office. It's good to have the people up front on your side but a person in a lateral position may be better able to

relate to your challenge. Remember, sometimes the most knowledgeable people are on your team. You can have a town hall meeting where you present the problem to the team and seek their advice. You will be awed with the wealth of information coming from the group. It is human nature to enjoy being asked for advice and when your team is asked to participate, it's a win-win. They are allowed to influence your decision while your influence with them is elevated.

- **Inspire.** There are times when a team knows what to do but action is slow due to their complacency. Maybe the day to day routine is no longer stimulating and the group has lost sight of their mission and purpose. When motivation lags, it is incumbent on you to become a cheerleader and inject a shot of energy into your group. Use your influence to get funding for an annual retreat with your team. At the retreat, make good use of the time to focus and re-commit to the important reasons that the group exists. Throughout the rest of the year, frequent communication used to review your greater purpose and reward individual success will inspire and motivate the entire group. Mobilizing around a compelling vision or purpose will energize your team. Above all else, make it a point as the leader to portray a positive and confident attitude. Use sincere personal warmth to connect with every individual and always make sure the team knows you expect them to be the best.

## End of Day Routine

## "The best way to ensure success tomorrow is to start today."

The end of the day is a special time and an opportunity to reflect on accomplishments, challenges and open items. Writing in *Business Insider*, author, Jessica Stillman notes that successful business CEO's have a routine for ending each day in a way that sets up success for the following day. As a healthcare leader, learn from other executives and develop a written plan for closing the day and then commit to it. Avoid the pitfall created by grabbing flash drives and folders on the way out the door in order to continue working at home. Evening work may occasionally be required if there's a crisis, but routinely working at home after a day on the job will quickly cause burn out. Finishing the day by reflecting on today and organizing for tomorrow is important and sets the stage for another productive day. Below are some points for developing your personal end of day routine.

- Block the last time slot on your calendar for EOD duties. Depending upon your position, you may need from 15 to 60 minutes to bring closure to the day and line things up for tomorrow.
- Begin your shut down routine by reviewing your today list. How did you do? Did you prioritize and were you able to cross off the most important items? What are the most important open items to transfer to the top of tomorrow's task list?
- Respond to necessary email and delete the unimportant items. Return phone calls and close as many pending conversations as possible.
- De-clutter your desk and your computer. Remove all notes and scraps of paper as well as every item in your in box that

can be quickly resolved.  Sign and send anything that requires your signature.
- Close your eyes and take a few minutes to review your leadership in a calm and objective way.  Use asset based thinking to recall the day's challenges and how tasks could have been approached differently.  Give thought to those who helped you as well as opportunities you may have had to help others.
- Thank somebody.  Gratitude is never frivolous and is essential for creating team prosperity.  A simple thanks pays large dividends when the person feels that their effort is appreciated. Thankfulness puts you in a positive frame of mind and helps you to appreciate the things that other people do to support your work.   Sometimes forgiveness or giving an apology can be as important as gratitude.
- Make the to-do list for tomorrow.  Although you may need to modify the list when you arrive in the morning, reviewing your calendar for upcoming appointments and starting with a list of things to be accomplished will allow you to efficiently start the new day.
- Go home and leave work at work.  You do not impress anyone if you're burned out by shuffling papers or working at the computer until everyone else is OTD.  In fact, it may even be viewed as a sign of inefficiency.  A successful leader is organized to the point that they can leave on time and leave the work at work.

Develop the end-of-day routine that works for you, your family activities and your personal life.  View it as a job requirement and use it consistently.  My personal EOD mantra is, **"CROTE." C**lean, **Re**flect, **O**rganize, **T**hank you, **E**xit.

# The Nutshell

### Your Leadership Skills Are In The Bag

**Woods** are used to get the game going. Put your leadership in motion by using the driver to establish and *share your vision* and reach for the other woods to *make a small difference immediately*. Long term vision and making early changes at the beginning of your leadership will connect you with your team and *leading by example* puts you half way down the fairway in a position for the next shot. These skills establish the environment for the beginning of your leadership while keeping the end in sight.

Pull out your **irons** to bridge the distance between your current position on the course and your final destination. The long iron will help you *organize your time and space* as you set the example for desired behavior. Judicious use of the short iron will *influence others*. The momentum you build with these two skills will carry you to a successful finish.

*Empowering, engaging and energizing* the team can be accomplished with your pitching **wedges**. This skillset opens the door to group creativity, allowing you to loft the team over any obstacles in the course of the day. By unleashing the power of the 3 E's you and your team will be in a position to put the final touch on any project.

The **putter** is used to cross the last few feet and make a direct hit with the target. A leader must guide the team toward the target and bring closure to each project. Closure happens after recognition has been given to the team and the *end of day routine* has been observed.

There is no single skill that guarantees your success in leadership. There are many skills and a multitude of occasions in which to use them. Invest your time and effort in developing as many leadership skills as possible. Fine-tune them, use trial and error, make your skills an integral part of your leadership while knowing that the more you practice, the easier the shots will become. A big bagful of single leadership skills will consistently produce a hole-in-one.

# Chapter 5

# Developing The Mission

## Lead With Purpose

Leading your team to a destination requires a map and a compass. Without them you will be treading water. Faced with high demands each day, healthcare leaders find it too easy to set aside the guide in order to deal with the crisis at hand. But leaders who are secure in their core values will have a plan with a purpose, knowing that the "mission with a vision" will see you through even in the midst of your most chaotic days.

Mission, Vision, Purpose, and Core Values are central in expert management. The mission statement of the organization is so vital that your acceptance of it may be required on your job contract or credentialing papers. At first glance, these four concepts appear to be similar and leaders sometimes use them interchangeably. Although Mission, Vision, Purpose and Core Values all provide direction, there are important, subtle differences.

- **Mission Statement** says why the organization exists. It sets priorities and tells the entire local population and global communities what you hope to achieve.
- **Vision** is a description of your future state. The successful leader teaches the team to understand the vision that they embrace and share.

- **Purpose** is the clarification and focus of the vision. It explains why you are going to the future state.
- **Core values** are the internal principles that guide your behavior. Your core values establish expectations as to how you behave and interact within your team. By following a common set of core values, your team members will hold one another accountable for behavior.

It's common for your organization's web page to have an "about" tab that describes the organization and provides the mission statement. To be an effective leader, access the web site to become aware of the values that you will be expected to adopt and support. As a leader, the time and energy you spend bringing mission, vision, purpose and values to life within your group will pay significant dividends.

## Mission statement

*"A mission is like a magnet that draws you to action."*

Effective mission statements are short and easy to remember. They are clear, concise and memorable using as few words as possible, frequently 15-25 words. In highly engaged and productive organizations, the mission is well known by all employees regardless of the job they do, for example:

- **The Cleveland Clinic:** To provide better care of the sick, investigation into their problems and further education of those who serve

- **New York Public Library:** To inspire lifelong learning, advance knowledge and strengthen our communities
- **American Red Cross:** (To)prevent and alleviate human suffering in the face of emergencies by mobilizing the power of volunteers and the generosity of donors
- **The Mayo Clinic:** To inspire hope and contribute to health and well-being by providing the best care to every patient through integrated clinical practice, education and research

Mission statements are important to you as a healthcare leader. You are in a position of trust within the organization and upper leadership expects your team to be aligned with the greater purpose of the organization. Although mission statements are general in nature, if the statement has been thoughtfully developed and phrased, it will provide a level of clarity to the working environment that exists throughout the organization.

## Vision statement

*"Vision without action is a dream. Action without vision is a nightmare."* Japanese proverb

There is a distinction between a solid leader and a quality manager. *Managers* determine the efficiency of the work group by completing designated tasks, scheduling, ordering supplies, and submitting payroll and performance reviews. A skilled manager is important and praiseworthy. *Leaders* function beyond management duties by having and implementing a vision. In addition to ensuring that managerial duties are performed, leaders are tasked with providing direction and constantly moving the group forward.  A leader provides focus and increases engagement within the group by developing and sharing the vision.  A skilled leader is the catalyst for positive change.

In addition to a mission statement, most organizations have a stated vision in which they set out a broad view of where the organization is going.  Organizations that know the value of a common vision will have the statement displayed throughout the facility.  Here are some examples of vision statements.

- **Smithsonian:** Shaping the future by preserving our heritage, discovering new knowledge, and sharing our resources with the world
- **Boy Scouts of America:** To prepare every eligible youth in America to become a responsible, participating citizen and leader who is guided by the Scout Oath and Law
- **San Diego Zoo:** To become a world leader at connecting people to wildlife and conservation
- **Baylor, Scott & White Healthcare:** To be the most trusted name in giving and receiving safe, quality, compassionate health care

One of the most important things that you can do as a leader is to develop a team vision.  The team vision must be known well enough that each person can recite it without thinking and it must be in alignment with that of the organization.  Ethically, you need to use the principles from the mission and vision of the organization and make them meaningful to your team.  A common vision promotes collaboration, creativity and a better appreciation for one another.

When the team members share the same purpose and trust each other, they will strive for a mutually beneficial outcome.

A good vision statement is more than an optimistic written wish; it should describe the future state. The statement must be practical, powerful, attainable and the result of team effort.

**Tips for developing a vision statement**

- **Listen and learn.** Develop a VS that the workgroup can relate to and embrace. Meet with your team to discuss the greater mission of the organization. Introduce your personal vision and listen to the team's thoughts, take notes and ask for feedback. Meet again to review the feedback and work together to turn *your vision* into a *common vision* that flows from that of the organization. Combine a greater goal with the specific tasks that you plan to accomplish and keep everything within the needs of your team members. Remember, your team must be able to see your vision through their eyes.
- **Define the desired outcome.** A common trap that leaders fall into while developing a vision statement is focusing on tasks rather than on desired outcome. In the chaos of daily routine, it is easy to focus on more efficiently doing tasks while losing sight of why we are doing them. By definition, a vision statement gives a picture of the desired future.
    - A bread company may have the vision of increasing sales or producing the product more efficiently. A better vision would include the community's enjoying and benefiting from their product.
    - A custom drapery company may have a vision of making blinds for windows of all sizes and shapes. A

better vision would include giving the customer control over light and privacy.
    - A busy ICU may have a vision of reducing death rates. A better vision would be restoring health to the individual while maintaining the emotional wholeness of the family
- **Engage your group in the process.** Using your leadership skills to guide the group in the process of creating the group vision will elevate your status as their leader and, consequently, team participation will increase regarding buy-in and engagement. Ideally, you would be allocated the necessary resources to pull your team out of the workplace for a team retreat. If not, a practical solution would be a series of town hall meetings where you could review the organizational vision, share your personal ideas and engage the group in developing a vision statement that will take them into the future.
- **Look beyond the daily tasks.** When working with your team to develop a vision statement, look beyond the tasks that are to be accomplished daily. Include concepts such as elevating one another as well as your community as a part of your team vision. Doing so will increase collaboration within the team as well as give you a sense of being connected to the community that you serve.

**Story lesson** At a meeting in San Francisco I met an anesthesia provider whose team had a vision for improving their health so that they could be better role models for their patients. Several of the team members started jogging before work, taking the same course every day. They always passed the same homeless people and started saying "good morning." As winter approached, the joggers gave their new acquaintances warm coats and before long, two of the displaced persons expressed an interest in exercising with the group. The healthcare workers chipped in and gave them new running shoes, and soon other homeless joined the group. Over time, the new joggers regained their health, their pride and their sense of worth. Thanks to the interest that was shown in them by the healthcare team members with a vision to improve their personal health and their community, several of the homeless now have jobs and homes, and a vision of their own.

## Purpose

*"Meet with your team and develop a shared purpose."*

If you think you have problems building consensus and motivating a team, consider the challenge faced by Coach Mike Krzyzewski when he agreed to coach the Olympic men's basketball team. Taking a group of millionaire all-stars and asking them to give up their summer vacations in order to play even more basketball was not an easy task. To be successful, the team needed a common purpose. Coach K took the team on a consciousness-raising trip to the tomb of The Unknown Soldier in Arlington Cemetery and talked about people giving their lives for their country. He then took the team to the area of the cemetery where recent casualties are buried and they viewed gravestones of people younger than they. He continued their training with workouts at the military academies where young people were preparing to give all for their country if necessary. When all was done, the team was no longer playing summer basketball; they were playing for the honor of their country and for all those who have given their lives to defend it. They had a common purpose.

Vision and purpose are similar concepts and both are important to the success of your team. Whereas vision looks into the future and is a compass for long range decisions, purpose tells us why we are going there. At Disney World, regardless of the employee's job description, their purpose as a team is to make sure that the customer's experience meets or exceeds their expectations. A common purpose for healthcare workers could be to reduce illness while promoting health, safety and satisfaction for both the patient and the family. By continuing to meet with your team and developing a shared purpose, engagement will grow as will scores on patient satisfaction surveys. Supporting the vision by actually implementing the purpose will remind your team on a daily basis where they are going and why it is important to get there.

Stepping back and identifying a purpose will help you in the workplace as well as in your everyday life. This book was a concept in my head for a long time before I sat down to write. My first writing sessions were a struggle and produced thoughts that did not always move smoothly from one to the next. Clearly, the project was not going as planned. In a brainstorming session with my wife, Liz asked, "What is the purpose of the book?" As we talked back and forth, I told her about my passion to help healthcare workers at all levels to become successful leaders. The book took shape following that discussion, and the words started spilling out. Whenever you sense that things are not going smoothly, step back and define the purpose.

# Core values

> *"Core values are based on respect and civility while promoting discovery and excellence. "*

New leaders often have problems establishing rules for the team because they're worried about getting pushback or being unpopular. Be assured that your team welcomes reasonable rules to promote collaboration and civility. Repeatedly, when workgroups are asked to describe the ideal leader, they want a person who establishes rules that apply to workers equally. Working with vague guidelines or inconsistent application of rules is a recipe for failure, theirs and yours.

When you establish the rules and develop the code of conduct, use the core values of the institution to provide a solid foundation. Core values are based on respect and civility while promoting discovery and excellence. Demonstrating those values will set the tone for how the entire group interacts with one another.

**Lesson**  A surgeon in a fast-paced surgery center had developed a reputation for being slow, highly critical of others and generally a grump. The support team found him so off-putting that they always warned a new frontline provider of the anticipated working conditions when that surgeon was assigned at the clinic. One day the surgeon had six cases, and the new provider who was assigned to him was also forewarned 24 hours in advance. Everyone came to work feeling anxious, subdued but on edge. The surgeon set a slow pace and negative tone before the first case and by late morning, with four cases remaining, the staff was worn from the surgeon's constant criticism and self-centeredness. But by early afternoon the doom-and-gloom morning improved. During lunch the anesthetist and the OR nurse had a brief constructive discussion in order to understand the surgeon's behavior and to develop a strategy to adjust the surgeon's attitude. The discussion worked and the two team mates changed the tone of the room to be more upbeat collaborative. Not only did the surgeon relax during the afternoon cases, but he later told the OR team, "Thank you. I had a great day!"

Core values are a reflection of the mission statement and should set a tone of civility and equal opportunity while promoting excellence in clinical practice. So often, we read and endorse the core values of the institution, but, we don't take the next step by making them a priority when interacting with our colleagues and patients. Ask yourself, "Does our behavior reflect those values?" Hospital web sites commonly identify the following as their core values.

- Respect
- Collaboration
- Innovation/discovery
- Accountability
- Integrity
- Excellence
- Diversity
- Stewardship

Meet with your team often and share your expectations. By soliciting your team for their opinions and involving them with the development of the culture, they are more likely to embrace it and to throw you their support. Here are some suggestions for rules of conduct.

**Respect one another.** Expecting workers to report on time and give full effort shows that people respect one another. Chronic late arrival shows a lack of respect for the job, your colleagues and for you as a leader.

Ask the workers to show respect for their peers by recognizing the unique set of skills each brings to the group and by acknowledging their contributions. Welcome their feedback and put aside the natural tendency to be defensive. As team members become more comfortable with the concept of a shared vision and purpose, they will appreciate and may welcome constructive commentary.

**Interact with civility.** Much has been written about the human brain having both emotional and thinking centers. Unfortunately, our brains are designed to react with fight or flight before the thinking brain kicks in. Your group, like all others, will have situations arise that push the button in the emotional brain. We can't control the unexpected but we can be held accountable for how we respond to it. As a leader, it is reasonable for you to expect that your team members pause to let the thinking brain kick in and then respond with civility when the unexpected occurs. Under no circumstances should you tolerate cursing, shouting, sarcasm or demeaning words. Being dismissive is the ultimate incivility.

**Never criticize a teammate.** The morale of your team deteriorates quickly when team members criticize one another. As a leader, it is your job to have difficult conversations and give critical feedback. When team members are allowed to criticize one another publicly, factions develop within the team and collaboration breaks down. If a team member has a concern, they should voice it with you and have confidence that you will follow-up. Remember, factions create fractures.

Keep in mind that you live under the hypocrisy microscope and any deviation from your own ethical standards will be noted by the team. It is essential that as a leader, you follow the rules that you set. "Do as I say, not as I do!" did not work when you were growing up yesterday, and it will not be tolerated by your team today.

## Team Meetings

*"Conducting a successful meeting is a learned skill. "*

Team meetings are a natural outcome of the effort to teach mission, vision, purpose and the use of core values in the healthcare workplace. You need meetings to develop the vision, to promote collaboration and elevate morale, to disseminate information and to discuss implementation of policy. Using core values to conduct meetings is central to your leadership.

Planning a productive meeting requires preparation with a purpose and clear objectives. Make the most of your time by posting the agenda ahead of time so that those attending the meeting are able to plan. Scheduling a meeting and then grabbing a handful of memos to read is a recipe for disaster.

**Story** Unhappy with the level of productivity from several previous meetings with my upper level management team, I opted to organize an agenda that included time blocks and a change of format. After presenting the topic for discussion, each member of the team was given 2 minutes to share as many thoughts on the topic as they could, after which the appointed timer moved to the next person. All thoughts were written on the board, and by continuing to ask, "What else?" the responses became more creative. After reviewing the thoughts, each person was given another 2 minutes to voice what they felt were the best options and to explain their choices. Following two rounds of reviews, the team was left with 3 viable solutions and quickly agreed on a plan of action that would achieve our goal. By planning with a purpose, adhering strictly to the new format and requiring that each person participate, the group found and committed to an answer that was better than any of them could have developed independently.

**Select a site.** Select a location that is large enough to accommodate the size of your group. A team of 30-50 may need a large classroom or small auditorium whereas gathering around a conference table might generate better discussion for a group of 10-15. The conditions of the room should also be considered - temperature, lighting and an adequate writing surface for each person.

**Who's invited?** Based on your objectives and agenda, consider who should be included in the meeting. When the purpose is to give general announcements to an entire department, everyone should be invited. If the focus of the meeting is on a single issue, a smaller workgroup would be more appropriate. After you determine your purpose, make sure all participants receive an invitation, consider where each person should sit and decide what each should bring and how each should prepare?

**Valuable tips for conducting a successful meeting**

- **Give reasonable notice** for all scheduled team meetings. Unless there is an urgent issue to be discussed, calling a last-minute meeting can create hardships. If you're working around a busy clinical schedule, do not plan to start too early or keep people too late before or after a shift.
- **Start and finish on time.** When posting the meeting, clearly state both the start and finish time and be prompt at both ends. Your team has a life outside your workplace and holding them over shows a lack of respect for their lives.
- **Have a printed agenda** for the meeting. Designate a period of time for each item on the agenda and keep on schedule. Allow time on the agenda for discussion of topics and also allow time for questions at the end.
- **Don't allow your meeting to be hijacked.** There are two common ways that a team meeting can be hijacked. The first is by a person who comes to the meeting with an issue that is not on the agenda. Often, it is a personal grievance that they want to make public. If you allow it, the new topic will dominate the meeting and your agenda will not be completed. Be assertive as a leader; stay on point and keep the meeting on schedule. Thank the person for verbalizing the concern and offer to meet with them privately. Assure them that if the problem has general interest, it will be included on the agenda for a future meeting. The second way that your meeting can be hijacked is by a few verbose individuals dominating the conversation. It's your job to limit discussion. Let them know that you appreciate their input, "…now let's hear from someone else."
- **Ban technology.** A person focused on a mobile device is not fully present or participating in the meeting. Establish a

standing rule that all mobile devices must be silenced and put away for the duration of the meeting.
- **Show appreciation.** All healthcare teams have schedules to keep and many have patients requiring their care. Often, your team meeting is an extra demand on their time. Always express your appreciation for their attendance and participation.
- **Clarify next step action items.** If agenda items are put into motion and team members are expected to follow through, re-state and clarify who is to do what and the timeline associated with all action.
- **Follow up.** People who invest their time in the team want ROI. Some items require action after the meeting so follow up promptly. I repeat, when the promised follow-up is not forthcoming, the team quickly learns that the meetings are all talk and no action. Timely follow-up shows respect.

It's not unusual for some leaders to limit meetings in order to avoid conflict. Remember, face time is important for you as a leader. Though current technology makes it easy to send group messages with announcements or policy changes, resist the temptation to use technology as a substitute for time with your team. You will appear to be hiding behind the techno wall and distant from your team. By openly discussing issues in a public forum, you provide transparency and you open the door to the greatest benefit of having a meeting – listening.

**Listen to the team.** The one and only way to truly understand the concerns of your team is to listen. When you have a 30-minute meeting and spout out 30 minutes of announcements and instructions, you walk away learning nothing from the group. Respect and appreciate that your team of frontline workers are the experts and they know the job better than anybody else. By listening to them and their concerns, you will gain advanced warning about problems just over the horizon. Plan your agenda with a limited number of topics for discussion. Present the topic to the group as quickly as possible and then close your mouth and listen. Thank and affirm each participant. To be more inclusive, direct questions to the less outspoken members of the group and draw out their thoughts.

As with all areas of leadership, conducting a successful meeting is a learned skill. Entire workshops are available that teach methods for interacting effectively. Among them is my leadership site www.prosynex.com included at the end of the book. Elevate your success by attending a leadership workshop or obtaining personal coaching.

## The Nutshell

***Sonja's Success* Story**   Sonja is the manager of a busy ambulatory surgery center. She is a new leader who is self-taught and routinely does many of the things listed in this chapter. Because the team is relatively small, she works clinically in addition to her management job. By continuing frontline work with patients, Sonja is able to role-model the behavior that is expected of the team and has the opportunity to interact with each person on an individual basis. Each morning the team meets for 5-10 minutes in the break room where they quickly review the day and receive updates about any administrative or clinical changes. On the wall of the break room are posters with the mission, vision and core values of the organization. Having them visibly posted keeps them in the front of everybody's mind each time they enter the break room. Several times per month Sonja assembles the team in the afternoon after all the cases are done and conducts a team meeting that may last up to an hour. She uses this time to welcome and listen to the thoughts of each individual, keeping in mind the mission, vision, purpose and workflow. As a result, she is well-respected by a team of highly motivated and competent professionals who consistently help one another. Morale is clearly high and patients respond with high satisfaction scores. Sonja gets high marks in the following areas.

- **Avid learner.** Although never formally trained as a leader, Sonja constantly seeks to improve her leadership skills. She reads management and team building books and seeks mentoring discussions with other experienced leaders.
- **Knows the vision.** By placing posters of the mission, vision and values of the organization where they can be seen daily by the team, Sonja has provided foundational expectations for the group.
- **Role-models.** Role-modeling is the best way to earn respect. The group clearly knows that she will not ask them to do anything that she doesn't do herself.
- **Communication.** A common mistake for new leaders is the assumption that a team of qualified professionals will always do the right thing. Often, team members want to do the right thing but boundaries have never been defined. By meeting daily with her team, she not only keeps them informed but she also has a forum for establishing boundaries.

I challenge you as a leader reader and as a learner of leadership: Be like Sonja. Know the mission and vision of the organization and build your vision around it. Unite with your team to elevate and sustain morale. Take the four standards of MVPC to your meetings and conduct a planned agenda that serves the purpose. Be responsible for connecting individually and collaboratively with your team and role-model the rules of conduct while taking active responsibility for ongoing learning. By customizing these concepts to meet any level of leadership, civility is established and Sonja's 'success story' will be yours.

# Chapter 6

# Recapping Leadership

"You've got to have a dream…if you don't have a dream, how ya gonna have a dream come true!!" – *South Pacific, the movie*

The world is full of dreamers, however, the world is *changed* by those who can turn a dream into a vision, develop a plan and follow through with the required action to make the dream a reality. The pathway to effective leadership begins with a dream and it is up to you to define the vision, convert it to a plan and bring it to life through action.

## Dream – Vision – Plan – Action

Whether we're developing a plan for the day or a plan for life, we start with a vision that anticipates evolving into an outcome. A single dad who is multi-tasking has a short-term vision that the clinic will close on time and that he will be able to attend his daughter's ballet recital. The child progressing from T-ball to little league may have a long-term vision of being an all-star major league player. But though his vision is firmly in place, life happens and things seldom go exactly as expected. By remaining true to the vision and by regarding the unexpected twists in the road as opportunities, visions do come to life in surprising ways and goals are achieved.

Turning a vision into a plan requires action and new skills may need to be learned in order to implement the plan. Dribbling a basketball is a skill that is easily learned, however, learning to dribble two basketballs at the same time requires a lot more concentration and effort. Learning to juggle balls in the air requires an expanded set of skills that are attained only through a dedication to learning and practice. Likewise, becoming an effective leader requires that you learn successively more complex skills as you progress from novice to commander in chief. When you started your first job and observed the behavior of your boss, you received your first lesson in dribbling the leadership ball. As your career progressed and you were given projects and tasks in addition to your normal work, you got your first lessons in dribbling two balls at the same time. Now you are a leader and you have an opportunity to take your skill set to the next level by learning to juggle. You can do it! Learning and following the advice in *Leader Reader 1* will give your leadership career a jump start.


## Place value on being inclusive

Chapter 3, Pathways to Leadership, reinforces the value of being inclusive. Not only do people take different paths to leadership, they take different paths to becoming a healthcare professional. One road leads to a medical degree while another may lead to nursing. Other healthcare pathways lead professionals to work as physician assistants, nurse practitioners, university faculty, x-ray technicians, blood bank technicians and many other necessary support positions. Healthcare Administration has leaders at all levels who may not be credentialed healthcare providers but play an important role in the day to day operation of the organization and the development of talent. Elevate yourself as a leader by realizing that there are no unimportant jobs or people in your organization. Rather than adopting an "us-versus-them" mentality, make a commitment to expand your support network to include people from as many areas as you can, and value the wealth of talent that each contributes to the organization.

Looking within your selected profession, you will find people who share the same license that you have but have very different abilities. As a new faculty member teaching Nurse Anesthesia, I felt secure thinking I was equipped with all the newest information and that I had the ability to be an effective teacher. Among the faculty was a person toward the end of his career who had not remained current, making me question why he remained on the teaching team. I quickly learned that what he lacked in textbook knowledge, he made up for in his ability to problem-solve and to simply get the job done. He was, for instance, the only person I'd heard of who had administered a general anesthetic inside an army tank! His relaxed personality and technical excellence made him a magnet for eager students who needed the confidence he offered them. My point? As a leader you will have some on your team who you may feel are less qualified than others. But by viewing every member of your team as having something valuable to contribute, and having the humility to acknowledge it, you will find hidden treasures on your team and build a workplace that has synergy.

Healthcare has a long history of attracting highly competent people who become sequestered within their own profession and work in parallel rather than in collaboration with other professions. Working in professional silos creates an adversarial attitude that gives rise to the cliche that "nursing would be a great profession if not for the docs" and vice versa. The new trend in healthcare – and let's work to make it a lasting one - is to promote patient safety and enhance patient outcomes by breaking down professional barriers and promoting collaborative interaction between professions. Moving forward in the 21$^{st}$ century, you will not be able to succeed as a healthcare leader unless you are able to cross professional lines and work collaboratively with everyone at every level in the organization. Networking skills as described in this book will open the door to becoming a part of the patient-centered healthcare workforce of the future.

Effective communication is an essential skill for working across professional lines and for maximizing the productivity of your team. Businesses have failed, wars have been lost and patients have died because of poor communication. Learning to communicate clearly and being able to deliver both good and bad news will determine your effectiveness as a leader. Because of its importance, communication skills will be explored in greater detail in *Leader Reader 2*.

## Who you are as a person matters

During my military career, the myriad of rules and regulations were sometimes confusing and conflicting, leaving an individual to question what was actually expected. I learned very early as a junior officer to observe and respect the unwritten rule of "command emphasis" when deciding the best course of action. Command emphasis was understood as "the behavior role modeled by the commander" and "when in doubt, follow the leader" was usually a safe way to proceed. Now you are the leader and the values you role-model are the ones that will be imitated. The way in which you interact with your team sends a louder message than any policy or procedure that you have on the books.

Values are extremely important and will influence the level of trust that your team places in you as their leader. You will excel as a leader when you build your personal leadership style on the foundation of integrity, honesty, transparency and fairness. What you do speaks louder than what you say and you must choose both your words and behavior carefully while keeping true to the values you profess. The integrity that you role model will give your team a sense of certainty and security. You are under the spotlight and will be most successful when you view your position on the stage as an opportunity to set high expectations through your own action.

A theme throughout this book is that success is built upon success and that theme is also applicable to the values that are evident in your team. Developing a team that embraces a solid set of core values starts during the interview and hiring process where you can create expectations and select only those who affirm your team's values. Hiring new staff based solely on their credentials may fill a hole in your schedule but may not give you a person who shares your principles. Adding a new member to your group is your opportunity to ensure that the applicant's credentials, attitude and values are all a match for you and your team. Lead with a focus on building the right team.

## Observe to learn, Listen to understand

One of the greatest mistakes that you can make as a leader is believing that you are the "information station" and that those above and below you on the chain of command are all eagerly waiting for you to impart your knowledge.  In addition to having a false sense of your own worth, that attitude will isolate you from those you lead as well as your potential mentors.  Your strength as a leader is not in the answers you bring to the position but in your ability to collaborate with those around you to find the best answer. Observing those around you will give you insight into how things can be accomplished. Listening will you give you an understanding of why things work.

The popular TV show *Who Wants To Be A Millionaire?* asks the contestant progressively more difficult questions.  When in doubt, the contestant has the option of using lifelines to gain more information and can choose between asking an expert, asking a friend or polling the audience.  Each option is viable and each is associated with a different level of success.  As a leader who has developed a support network, you have options just like the TV show contestant.

- Experts abound in a hospital and can be consulted to address your problem.  Although they may be an expert in their area, they are not familiar with your workplace or the nuances of your team.  On the TV show experts are correct about 50% of the time.
- Mentors are friends who know your background and a little about your job and the problems you face.  They tend to be well-rounded and offer sound advice.  On the TV show friends (mentors) are correct about 65% of the time.
- The collective wisdom of your team is the equivalent of polling the audience.  Your team works side by side with you and fully understands the workplace as well as the nature of the challenge that is being faced.  Having a team meeting

and listening to their opinions is the valuable equivalent of polling the audience.  On the TV show polling the audience is correct a whopping 95% of the time.

Observing and Listening are easily facilitated by having town hall meetings with the whole team.  It's also a great way to elevate yourself as a leader because in addition to finding creative solutions to ongoing problems, you will build cohesion and trust within the group.  *Leader Reader 2* takes a closer look at the importance of effective listening when building trust within team.

## Courage Builds Courage

Leadership takes courage and, ironically, builds courage as you successfully address challenges.  Confronting problems head-on, stating what needs to be said, making decisions, and holding people accountable all take courage and all are necessary.  Two actions to take as soon as possible after becoming a leader are, 1) connecting with your team and, 2) building a network of people who will support you as you face challenges.  Connecting individually and collectively with your team is a grass-roots theme throughout this book and is absolutely essential in building and maintaining a collaborative and trusting team.

Despite best intentions, human interaction is not always smooth.  By building a trusting relationship with your team and valuing each individual, you will receive your team's support through the good times and the challenging ones.  Connect with them, show your ongoing appreciation for the talent they bring to the job and when it's time to step up, they will be there.

Developing a wide network of supportive colleagues will increase the likelihood that you know someone who has solved a similar problem. If you spend all your time within your workplace and limit yourself to interacting only with your team, you will cut yourself off from the collective wisdom of the organization. As you take action to lead change, develop a network to get the benefit of knowing what has worked in other areas.

When we think of change, we frequently think of new things that can be implemented to improve workflow, patient care or team morale. There are times when the nature of the organization changes significantly and a choice must be made to compromise one's own values or leave the organization. At one point in my career the entire chain of command above me was changed and the new boss implemented a workflow contrary to the job that I was originally hired to do, more importantly, contrary to my values. It took courage to know that I could not be effective in the new environment and to move on.

## Go forward with confidence

Effective leadership starts with a dream, gains focus with a vision, takes on purpose with a plan and is manifested in reality through the engaged action of the team. In business and healthcare communities alike new leaders emerge at all levels of responsibility with hopes of engaging the team and moving the success of the company forward. New equally intelligent and competent leaders are frequently asked to motivate and empower their teams as part of their job description. Many are enormously successful while others seem challenged to provide the most basic management skills. So what allows one new leader to soar while the other struggles? It is, highly probable that the successful leader manifested many of the traits and skills described in *Leader Reader 1*, whereas the less successful person gained a leadership title before developing leadership skills, or without knowing how. Regardless of your skill level in leadership, when you are entrusted with a leadership position, your ultimate success is more closely tied to your commitment to learning and doing than to your entry level knowledge. Commit to learning, anticipate success and be like Katie.

My younger brother, Jim, had four children and as they were growing, he did not allow them to use the words, "I can't." He stressed that even though they couldn't do something yet, they would learn as they grew. His ban on "I can't" planted the seed for anticipation of future success. I clearly remember the day when I asked 4-year-old Katie whether or not she could tie her shoes. "I've not yet learned to do that," was the reply. Katie is currently a highly competent oncology nurse who, not surprisingly, was able to tie her shoes well before she entered kindergarten!

As you make the transition from worker to leader, don't forget the dream. Somewhere inside you there is still a hopeful dreamer who made a leap of faith into leadership. As you dream and visualize and plan, do it with the anticipation of success.

## Acknowledge Others

Early in my military career when I was promoted to Captain, Col Nelson called me into his office. He explained that I would be taking on additional responsibility and offered a word of advice. He said, "Son, you can't push a rope. If you want to lead, go to the front and start pulling." With those words my leadership experience started and I remember the advice to this day.

As my leadership interest grew, I had the good fortune to work for many talented leaders in military and civilian hospitals. All were highly competent and most of them approached leadership by placing and emphasis on team building and collaboration. Their collective leadership styles have had a lasting influence on the style that I use in leadership positions. Many of the tips in this book originated from the behaviors that I observed in numerous excellent leaders throughout my career. They helped teach me what To Do.

In addition to great leaders, I can remember a few who were very poor leaders and I learned from them as well. One of the poor leaders had a total focus on self-promotion and regularly sacrificed team members whenever it served her cause. Another poor leader was a man who felt that he was personally responsible for the success of the organization and chose to micromanage to the point that the team was paralyzed with fear of taking any sort of initiative. They helped teach me what Not To Do.

Successful leaders are not born into their positions. Successful leaders progress through a lifetime of experience to arrive at a leadership position. Regardless of your background or your level of responsibility, there will be people along the way who influence and encourage you. You may know a respected leader, a teacher or a family member, but somewhere along the line someone who believes in you will encourage your growth. An essential component of integrity is acknowledging and thanking those from your past and in your present whose only motivation for supporting you is your success. Although I have learned from everyone I've worked with and for, here are some of the people who provided inspiration for this book.

## Give Gratitude

*Leader Reader 1* would not have taken form and been published without the unquestioned support given to me by my wife, Liz. Throughout my career, Liz has recognized my ability and encouraged me to take risks to expand my experience as a leader. She is an incredible project manager and source of inspiration. Without her editing ability and attention to timelines, this book would be an unfulfilled dream.

Dr. Timothy Bittenbinder, Anesthesiology Department Chair at Baylor, Scott & White, offered me a significant opportunity for leadership in a civilian hospital when he entrusted a large group of Nurse Anesthetists to my charge. It was in this environment that I developed a passion for leadership development. Many of the values described in this book were learned while working with Dr. Bittenbinder.

While at Scott & White Medical Center, I was offered additional leadership opportunity when asked to serve as the Chair of the Advanced Practice Council.  Dr. Robert Probe, Dr. Andre Avots, and Dr. Dudley Baker actively promoted the council and my leadership. In addition to the physicians named above, Laurie Benton, PA provided collaborative support and remains a friend.  Her opinions were valuable during the writing of this book.

The Johns Hopkins Division of Anesthesiology and Critical Care Medicine provided fertile learning ground at all levels of healthcare leadership.  I was appointed by Dr. Dan Nyhan, then Interim

Director of ACCM.  Dan faithfully maintained an open-door policy and his mentorship evolved into a lasting friendship.  At Hopkins I enjoyed the opportunity to mentor and teach leadership skills to a select group of rising stars who will become the future leaders of the Division.  As is commonly the case, mentoring is a two-way process and my personal leadership skills were enhanced by mentoring others.

During my tenure at The Johns Hopkins, I had the good fortune of establishing a friendship with Ken and Heather Jennings, founders of Third River Partners.  Ken's book, *The Serving Leader, Five Powerful Actions to Transform Your Team, Business, and Community* has affirmed many of my basic beliefs about leadership.  The follow-up book, *The Greater Goal, Connecting Purpose and Performance* added depth to my existing commitment to collaborative leadership.   I am especially thankful for the friendship and mentoring that I received from John Porcari, a valuable member of the Third River team and a respected Serving Leadership coach.

I am also thankful for my long time friend and colleague, Wilma Gillis, who is the Chief Nurse Anesthetist at the University of Wisconsin.  Over the years Wilma has always taken my calls and offered her insight when I faced leadership challenges.  Wilma freely gave her time in phone interviews and emails and helped by doing a pre-publication review of the information.  Some of the tips in this book came from Wilma.

A special thank you also goes out to the numerous people in leadership positions who shared their wisdom and offered their opinions while I was doing research and writing this book.  By openly sharing the leadership skills that make you successful, you validated much of the information in this book.  Special thanks go to Kimberly Westra, David Pennington, Jim Camp, Lynn Reede, Joe

Casey and my friend of 30 years, Dr. Paul Austin.  Although the book is published in my name, it reflects the collective wisdom of many people who have been friends, colleagues and former leaders throughout this part of my leadership journey. Thank you to all.


Take your team to the next level with leadership and team building coaching.   Contact Tom Davis to enhance your leadership ability and empower your team.

www.ProSynEx.com

tom@procrna.com

follow @procrnatom on Twitter for the latest on-line leadership articles.


## About Leader Reader Two

Leader Reader Two will continue your mentorship with discussions about everyday issues like hiring and firing, contract negotiations, interviewing, managing change and managing conflict.  It will expand on team meetings and emphasize team building.  The book will review values-based leadership and give you confidence about when to say yes, when to say no and when to say goodbye.

# References

The following are books that provide solid information and helped develop my leadership skills. Read, enjoy and let them broaden your knowledge base as you develop excellence as a leader.

- *Stumbling on Happiness,* Dan Gilbert
- *The Serving Leader: Five Powerful Actions to Transform Your Team, Business and Community,* Ken Jennings and John Shahl-Wert
- *Trust and Betrayal in the Workplace: Building Effective Relationships in Your Organization,* Dennis Reina and Michelle Reina
- *Crucial Conversations: Tools for Talking When Stakes are High,* Kerry Patterson, Joseph Grenny, Ron McMillan and Al Switzler
- *Never Split the Difference: Negotiating as if Your Life Depended On it,* Chris Voss and Tahl Raz
- *Start with No: The Negotiating Tools that the Pros Don't Want You to Know,* Jim Camp
- *The Greater Goal: Connecting Purpose and Performance,* Ken Jennings and Heather Hyde Jennings
- *The Power of TED,* David Emerald
- *Why Hospitals should Fly: The Ultimate Flight Plan to Patient Safety and Quality Care,* John Nance
- *If Disney Ran Your Hospital: 9 ½ Things You Would Do Differently,* Fred Lee
- *Turn the Ship Around: A True Story of Turning Followers into Leaders*

Made in the USA
Lexington, KY
18 April 2017